ENTREPRENEURIAL
EDGE

Essential Skills for Business Success

ENTREPRENEURIAL
EDGE

Essential Skills for Business Success

FALIH M. ALSAATY

ARPress

ILLUMINATING IDEAS.
EMPOWERING VOICES

ARPress LLC
45 Dan Road Suite 5
Canton MA 02021
Hotline: 1(888) 821-0229
Fax: 1(508) 545-7580

Ordering Information:
Quantity sales. Special discounts are available on quantity purchases by corporations, associations, and others. For details, contact the publisher at the address above.

Printed in the United States of America.

ISBN-13: Softcover   979-8-89330-336-0
           eBook   979-8-89330-337-7

Library of Congress Control Number: 2024900515

Table of Contents

Preface

The era of ChatGPT, artificial intelligence, disruptive innovation, and environmental dynamics poses a unique challenge to leaders of entrepreneurial business venture as they seek to achieve superior competitive advantage for their firms in a global marketplace. The challenge doesn't only stem from domestic and international competitors but also from other external sources such as man-made and natural disasters that are beyond the control of entrepreneurs or business leaders. While entrepreneurs seek to establish innovative, growth-oriented, and competitive ventures, business managers on the other hand pursue tasks to ensure the survival, profitability, and sustainability of business firms.

Entrepreneurship and the management of the entrepreneurial companies are comprised of interrelated activities and disciplines. Entrepreneurship and its management are fascinating subjects because they perform critical functions in society and occur within all industries, economic sectors, and countries. Entrepreneurs with strong managerial and leadership skills are likely to be highly successful in their endeavors.

This short book is about the basics of entrepreneurship and management. It is designed for individuals of different background including students, managers, business owners, entrepreneurs, and the public at large. The book seeks to address important issues related to the entrepreneurial ecosystem as well as explain essential matters and challenges that face the management of entrepreneurial companies. It is assumed that the reader has scant or no knowledge about entrepreneurship, management, U.S. industries, the economy, or the inner workings of business firms.

The book aims to accomplish several objectives:

Help readers learn the process of entrepreneurship and the principles of managing a business enterprise, including the intricacies of business strategies.

Overview the techniques and methods essential for business growth and achieving sustainable competitive advantage.

Enable readers to become successful entrepreneurs and effective business leaders.

The emphasis in this book is on business entrepreneurship. However, business as well as social entrepreneurs play an indispensable role in society for a host of reasons including job creation and contribution to national income. In recent years, an increasing segment of U.S. population has acquired the entrepreneurial mindset (or spirit) as evidenced by the growing numbers of new business firms[1]. This book provides a road map for starting a new venture, managing the venture, and growing the business.

---

1   In this book, the terms enterprise, corporation, small business, business firm, company, and business venture are used interchangeably.

To my family - with love and delight

Chapter 1
The Entrepreneurship Landscape

Learning Objectives
Entrepreneurial Mindset
Entrepreneurial Venture and Ecosystem
Entrepreneurship Theories and Technology
Nature and Contribution of Entrepreneurial Firms
The Cycle of Business Creation and Destruction
Entrepreneurial Success: Guidelines for Entrepreneurs
Chapter Summary
Chapter Questions

Chapter 2
Vision, the Product, the Market, and Competitive Advantage

Learning Objectives
Business Concept, Business Model, and the Business Plan
Business Plan Software
The Face-to-Face Interview
The Venture's Business Plan and Competitive Advantage
Executive Summary: An Example
Chapter Summary
Chapter Questions

Chapter 3
The Search for Venture Financing

Learning Objectives
Sources of Venture Funding
General Funding Guidelines
Chapter Summary
Chapter Questions

Chapter 1

The Entrepreneurship Landscape

"It's not about ideas. It's about making ideas happen."

Scott Belsky

Learning Objectives:

- Understand "entrepreneurship"
- Recognize the entrepreneurial process.
- Learn about the factors that impact business growth.
- Understand the entrepreneurship ecosystem.

Entrepreneurship is a process (a set of activities) about creating, managing, and growing business ventures to introduce innovative products and/or services in which entrepreneurs pursue the achievement of social goals (i.e., social entrepreneurship) or business goals (i.e., commercial entrepreneurship)[2]. A driving force of entrepreneurship is the entrepreneur's mindset which refers to the individual's vision, attitude, behavior, and skills. Entrepreneurship has become in recent decades an established academic discipline that embodies principles,

---

[2] There are many definitions of entrepreneurship because the concept is often viewed from different angles. For example, entrepreneurship is defined as "a discipline that seeks to understand how opportunities are discovered, created, and exploited, by whom, and with what consequences." See, Heidi, Neck M. et al (2018). *Entrepreneurship*, Sage Publishing, Los Angeles: California, p.6.

theories, techniques, and applications. As such, it is taught at the graduate and undergraduate levels in many colleges and universities in the United States and elsewhere around the world.

In the United States, the spirit of entrepreneurship is deeply rooted among millions of individuals, young and old, men and women. Some of them being first-time entrepreneurs. Others are second- or even third-time entrepreneurs. These individuals are called serial entrepreneurs because they are accustomed to repeating the process of establishing and growing business firms often for the purpose of selling them for profit. Whether the individual is a first-time or serial entrepreneur, entrepreneurship is about taking advantage of market opportunities. Opportunities reflect demand prospects for goods and services, domestically and internationally.

Entrepreneurial Mindset

The field of entrepreneurship is characterized by several important concepts that entrepreneurs ought to understand to achieve business success. Chief among these is the entrepreneurial mindset. California State University/Chico defines the mindset as "a set of beliefs, knowledge, and thought processes that equips people to recognize opportunities, take initiative, and succeed in diverse settings". The University indicates that the elements of the mindset are:

- Entrepreneurial critical thinking (also called creative or strategic thinking)
- Flexibility and adaptability
- Ability to communicate and collaborate.
- Willingness to take business risk.
- Initiative and self-reliance
- Forward or futuristic looking
- Opportunity seeking
- Creativity and innovation.

The task of entrepreneurs is to monitor, seek, analyze, and exploit opportunities. While some entrepreneurs focus their efforts on local or national markets because of limited resources available to them, others consider the larger globe as their target market. Alertness to opportunities is a key trait of successful entrepreneurs. Market opportunities are also vital for entrepreneurs (as well as for the country) because opportunities:

- Give rise to the introduction of new goods and services.
- Are the main reason for the emergence of new technologies and industries.
- Are the force behind inventions and innovations.
- Are the force behind the firms' revenue and profit.
- Are the motivating factors for the creation of entrepreneurial and other firms.
- Enhance the country's economic superiority and competitive advantage.

The question whether entrepreneurs are born or made has attracted the attention of scholars in the field of entrepreneurship for a long time. Specifically, are entrepreneurs born with entrepreneurial traits? Or can the traits be acquired through education, experience, desire, or some other means by the individual? Many experts believe that entrepreneurs are made and that the entrepreneurial talents and attributes can be acquired by individuals who possess the motivation and resolve to engage in entrepreneurial activity.

For example, Soni and Kanupriya (2021) believe that entrepreneurial intention (creativity, passion, and self-efficacy) plays a decisive role in the process of becoming an entrepreneur, and the prerequisite to establish a business venture. Yitshaki et al (2022) indicated that compassion is acknowledged as a key factor of opportunity recognition of social ventures startup. The question to be addressed here is: What are some of the notable traits of entrepreneurs? Entrepreneurs possess several business-related personality attributes, including the following:

- Seeing the world as having ample economic opportunities that need to be explored and exploited. The entrepreneur's vision is strategic, forward looking, and globally oriented.
- Thinking creatively and pursuing opportunities with innovative products or services

- Willingness to take on risk above and beyond ordinary levels.
- Communicating ideas, eagerness for networking, and skills for building sponsorship

Why do many individuals have the tendency and desire to become entrepreneurs?

The quest for entrepreneurship could be attributed to two main sets of factors: First, the personality attributes of individuals. And second, the impact of the external environment; for instance, looing market opportunities – that motivate pursuing the entrepreneurial path. Briefly, a larger set of factors may include the following[3]:

- To realize the individual's vision of being professionally and financially independent and free from being a subordinate to others
- To utilize one's education, knowledge, technical skills, expertise, or social network.
- To take advantage of an emerging economic opportunity
- To achieve wealth, fame, or both
- To lead family business or fulfil the family's dream.
- To network with society's "rich and famous"
- To gain organizational power and decision-making influence
- To bridge an economic, social, cultural, or technological need in society
- To attain political or social influence
- To satisfy a desire for risk taking
- To assist others via job creation and income generation.

Entrepreneurial Venture and Ecosystem[4]

---

3   Research findings indicate that there are a variety of motivational factors, reasons, and ideas for individuals to engage in entrepreneurial activity. See, for example, Muhammad, Naveed, L. and Ahmad, Maha (2022). The Entrepreneur's Quest: A Qualitative Inquiry into the Inspirations and Strategies for Startup in Pakistan, *Pakistan Economic and Social Review*, 58(1), 61-71.

4   The entrepreneurial activity is a major source of economic growth and prosperity in many countries. See for example, Gomes, Sofia and Ferreira, Pedro (2022). Entrepreneurial activity and economic growth: A dynamic data panel analysis of European countries, *Entrepreneurial Business and Economics Review*, 10(2), 7-20.

Entrepreneurial activity is the manifestation of the entrepreneur as the agent of change, invention, innovation, and economic progress. The entrepreneur becomes involved in many endeavors and tasks including the following:

- Creating a business venture to offer desired goods or services.
- Seeking appropriate sources of venture funding
- Deploying suitable technology for the venture
- Employing technical, financial, managerial, and other skills
- Managing the venture with vision, strategies, and leadership
- Meeting or creating the demand for the output.
- Growing the venture and expanding its market reach and technology base.

The entrepreneurial startup venture is usually a small business firm until it acquires more resources, penetrates additional markets, and grows larger. The size of a business firm[5] and its rate of growth can be measured in terms of employment, sales, assets, profits, or other measurement indicators. A small firm, therefore, can be defined differently depending on the criteria being used. In the United States, however, the U.S Small Business Act defines a small firm as "one that is independently owned and operated, and which is not dominant in its field of operation." On the basis of this definition, the U.S. Small Business Administration (SBA) considers a business enterprise to be "small" if it meets or is below the following size:

- 500 employees for most manufacturing and mining industries
- 100 employees for all wholesale trade industries
- $6.5 million of average annual revenue for most retail and service industries
- $31 million of average annual revenue for most general and heavy construction industries
- $13 million of average annual revenue for all special trade contractors

---

5   In this book, no distinction is made between small business firms and entrepreneurial firms, because U.S. official statistical data about business firms do not distinguish between these two sets of organizations. Similarly, no distinction is made between small business owners and entrepreneurs.

- $0.75 million of average annual revenue for agriculture industries.

Is it a good idea that a small business definition be different on the basis of the firm's industrial sector? Well, the SBA numerical approach to a small business definition is important for entrepreneurs to (i) know the actual place of their businesses in the hierarchy of business size classification in the country as (a) small, (b) mid-sized, and (c) large, and (ii) realize their eligibility or lack of it to apply for the SBA loan guarantee program and benefit from other services provided by the agency. It is to be noted that, in general, firms with employment of less than 20 individuals are called micro firms, while firms with employment of more than 500 employees but less than 1,000 are considered mid-sized, and firms with employment of more than 1,000 individuals are deemed large.

Often, dedicated small business owners gradually become entrepreneurs, or even series entrepreneurs, as time passes by adopting bigger and more ambitious business plans and pursuing projects that entail greater degrees of risk. The owners become more visionary, innovative, and aggressive in seeking opportunities. Entrepreneurs come up with new business ideas to introduce original, practical, appealing, valuable, cheaper, amusing, satisfying, or comforting products as these products are appreciated and bought by customers. Achieving customer fulfilment is the prime reason for entrepreneurial undertakings.

The entrepreneurship ecosystem refers to the entrepreneur and his/her external environment that includes societal culture, institutions, the market, and the economy. These factors, in aggregate, influence the extent and intensity of entrepreneurial activity. Kauffman organization (Kauffman.org) defines the term as "A network of people supporting entrepreneurs, and the culture of trust and collaboration that allows them to interact successfully." Moreover, "The speed at which talent, information, and resources move through the ecosystem can affect entrepreneurs at each stage in their lifecycle." In 2011, Professor Daniel J Isenberg introduced an innovative model that depicts the domain of the entrepreneurship ecosystem, comprised as follows: finance, culture, supports, human capital, markets, and policy. Specifically, the domain encompasses many factors that include the following:

- Leadership and government
- Human capital and networks
- Innovation centers and incubators
- Entrepreneurial education
- Capital markets
- Legal business environment
- Products, services, and markets.

Entrepreneurship Theories and Technology

As a body of knowledge, entrepreneurship derives its legitimacy form a host of theoretical foundations that have come to be known as entrepreneurship theories. Many theories came to existence during the past seven decades or so, rooted in the fields of economics, sociology, psychology, management, and other social sciences. The theories have enabled entrepreneurship to become a notable field of teaching, learning, and research. Colleges and universities in the United States and elsewhere offer undergraduate and graduate level studies in entrepreneurship nowadays, an indication that entrepreneurs can in fact "be made."

According to USC Libraries (libguides.usc.edu) "theories are formulated to explain, predict, and understand phenomena, and in many cases, to challenge and extend existing knowledge within the limits of critical bounding assumptions". As far as the entrepreneurship field is concerned, the most widely mentioned theories are indicated below (Simpeh, Kwabena, 2011; Cherukara and Manalel, 2011):

- Economic Entrepreneurship. The focus of this group of theories is on the role of entrepreneurs in the production, exchange, and distribution of goods and services.
- Psychological Entrepreneurship. The emphasis of this category of theories is on the personality characteristics of the entrepreneur

such as the tendency for risk taking, need for achievement, and tolerance for ambiguity.

- Sociological Entrepreneurship. This collection of theories stresses the importance of societal factors that pave the way for the emergence and activity of entrepreneurship. The factors include social networks, background of the individual entrepreneur, and the society's economic and political system.
- Anthropological Entrepreneurship. Anthropological theories treat the cultural attributes of a society as the main motivational factor the individual's intention and subsequent decision to engage in entrepreneurial activities.
- Opportunity-Based Entrepreneurship. The essence of this set of theories is that environmental changes such as economic, social, natural disasters, and the like create business opportunities in a country that give rise to entrepreneurship.
- Resource-Based Entrepreneurship. The position taken by this group of theories is that resource availability such as financial, technical, and managerial skills can make it possible for the individual to engage in entrepreneurial activities via the creation of business ventures.

A newly established entrepreneurial venture, like other progressive business firms, is in need for the deployment of technology to facilitate its operations and improve its performance. The venture's technology in its early stage of development should not be highly advanced or expensive. Rather, the technology needs to be appropriate, affordable, and operational. Scott Gerber (www.bplans.com), for example recommends the following technologies for entrepreneurial films:

- An Internal chat platform
- Project management software
- Password and credentials software such as LastPass
- Video equipment
- USB modems and scalable data plans
- A tech chat platform for team communication such as Slack
- Training software such as Lessonly
- Stress management software such as Pocket Yoga

- Rank tracker which a productivity tool that shows the company ranking in search engines.

Nature and Contribution of Entrepreneurial Firms

What are the main differences between entrepreneurial firms and traditional "mom-and-pop" or similar small firms? There are several key differences between the two kinds of businesses, as indicated below:

Technology. Entrepreneurial firms, unlike other small firms, are technology-oriented entities in the sense that their business model calls for the deployment of modern technology that includes machine learning and Artificial Intelligence (AI). This is especially true for market disruptors (e.g., disruptive innovation companies). Market disruptors usually attract venture capitalists and other investors who are willing to commit substantial amount of funding, and who assist the venture to go "public" via a stock offering.

Finance. As alluded to above, entrepreneurial firms are in general capable of generating substantial amount of initial and subsequent financing as startup ventures. For example, according to *2022 CNBC Disruptors*, Ryan Peterson, the founder and Chief Executive Officer (CEO) of the cloud computing company Flexport, stated the company raised $2.2 billion in funding.

Big Ideas. Entrepreneurs generally dream of "big" ideas and exert persistent efforts to translate them into new or improved goods or services ventures. Many entrepreneurs also seek to change the world to make it a better place with their invention or innovation. On the other hand, owners of traditional small firms are more inclined to owning a business that offers ordinary goods and services mainly to a local community or market. Examples include dentists, lawyers, plumbers, hair stylists, and countless convenient stores owners. Undoubtedly, the owners of these and other small establishments provide essential services to society and are likely to be content with their profession, scope of operations, and degree of business risk.

Geographic Horizon. Entrepreneurial firms are typically born with the intention to serve a broad segment of customers with the focus on both domestic and international markets. As they grow, the firms develop global business strategies augmented by greater resources, a worldwide labor force, and complex organizational structures. These firms have come to acquire different names: international corporations, global corporations, multinational corporations, multinational enterprises, and cross-national organizations. As indicated earlier, small ordinary firms, however, are established primarily to service a limited geographic horizon such as a local community.

Degree of Risk. Entrepreneurs, unlike the rest of the population, are willing to accept a greater degree of business risk in founding business firms. Of course, they also expect to obtain a higher level of compensation in the form of financial rewards.

What are the major contributions of entrepreneurial firms to the U.S. economy?

The private sector in general – and the entrepreneurial firm in particular – represents the strongest pillar of the U.S. economy[6] because of the indispensable role in providing one or more of the following:

- Employment creation
- Output production, assembly, delivery, and marketing
- Formation of new businesses and industries
- Introduction of new or improved technology and means of production and transportation.
- Income generation (e.g., wages, salaries, fringe benefits)
- Workforce training and professional development
- Exporting and importing of goods and services
- Financial and in-kind assistance to the society's needy
- Reinforcing the country's global economic and technological leadership.

6   Empirical findings show the existence of a positive relationship between entrepreneurship and economic growth in which entrepreneurship promotes economic growth of nations. See, Sabra, Mahmoud M. and Shreteh, Dalal (2021). The Nexus Relationship between Entrepreneurship and Economic Growth Dynamic: Evidence from Selected MENA Countries, *International Economic Policy*, 35, 56-75.

The U.S economy is an open market system with free movement of goods and services. It is the world's largest, most vibrant, and highly competitive economy. For example, the Bureau of Economic Analysis estimated the U.S. Gross Domestic Product (GDP) at $23.00 trillion in 2021. China, for comparison, ranked second in the world with a GDP estimated at $17.74 trillion, followed by Japan at $4.94 trillion, Germany at $4.22 trillion, the United Kingdom at $3.19 trillion, and India at $3.17 trillion.

The U.S. private sector is the dominant source of the economy's size, strength, and growth. The sector consists of thousands of firms in a variety of industries that employ millions of individuals. As shown in Table 1 below, the number of business establishments in the country was about eight million in 2019[7] with a workforce of 133 million people and an annual payroll of more than $7 trillion. It is interesting to note that micro firms (firms with less than 20 employees) comprised 69 percent of all establishments in the country in 2019, an indication that the U.S. is "a country of small businesses." The data also reflects the fact that the economy offers huge economic opportunities for well-conceived, innovative startups.

---

[7]   It was estimated that the number of U.S. businesses without employees was about 25 million in 2021.

Table 1

Size, Employment, and Payroll of Business Establishments in the United States, 2019[8]

Enterprises	Number of Firms	Number of Establishments	Employment	Annual Payroll ($1,000)	Percent of Total Establishments
Total	6,102,412	7,959,103	132,989,428	7,428,553,593	100
Less than 5 employees	3,777,085	3,783,930	6,003,770	294,917,415	48
5-9 employees	1,013, 629	1,026,898	6,681,959	267,500,052	13
10-19 employees	640,827	674,135	8,632,696	358,971,177	4
Less than 20 employees	5,431,541	5,484,963	21,318,425	921,388,644	69
20-99 employees	555,046	728,140	21,762,863	995,870,795	9
100-499 employees	94,957	375,232	18,612,620	1,008,135,146	5
Less than 500 employees	6,081,544	6,588,335	61,693,908	2,925,394,585	83
500 or more employees	20,868	1,370,768	71,295,520	4,503,159,008	17

Source: Census Bureau, https://www2.census.gov/programs-surveys/susb/tables/2019/us_state_6digitnaics_2019.xlsx, published on February 11, 2022.

The Cycle of Business Creation and Destruction

Business firms are expected to go through four stages in their life cycle: (1) birth, (2) growth, (3) decline, and (4) death[9]. Organizational life cycle is a phenomenon regardless of the firm's size or industrial sector. Some firms disappear from the marketplace because of a merger with or acquisition by other firms. However, firms can extend their life span via continual innovation, diversification, or both. U.S. published data show that the survival probability of a small business firm is very low, about 7 percent. This means that more than 90 percent of newly established startup ventures in the country will disappear from the marketplace in a relatively short period of time, typically between two and five years.

---

8   An establishment may consist of more than one firm.
9   Digitalsilk.com defines the business life cycle as "a cyclical representation of the stages an average business goes through from seeding to decline and renewal." The company also indicates that round 20 percent of startup ventures fail during the first year of operations.

The main causes of failure for the great majority of newly formed firms include poor leadership, insufficient critical resources, and lack of market demand for their products or services (see Table 2 for additional reasons). To minimize the probability of failure, and increase the likelihood for venture survival, the entrepreneur needs, among other things, to understand the product, the market, the industry, and the technology. However, the root cause of business failure in many instances rests on the shoulders of the entrepreneur and his or her management team. Authors have suggested that nascent entrepreneurial and other small firms fail for a host of reasons as indicated below[10]:

Table 2

Reasons for Small Firms Failure

Negative cash flow	Pursuing ineffective strategies
Failure to take advantage of new technology	Profit erosion
Overlapping managerial authority	Failure to exploit new market opportunities
Loss of key suppliers or customers	Lack of product differentiation
Rigid organizational culture and/or structure	Poor organizational communication
Lack of company vision	Lack of a cash cushion
Loss of managerial/technical critical skills	Poor customer relations
Hopeless leadership and/or internal conflicts	Low quality product
Failure to realize and learn from past mistakes	excessive reliance on borrowing
Poor risk management	Poor inventory management
Absence of planning	Mediocre pricing policy
Costly legal disputes	Inability to control expenses
Inability to compete	Overreliance on single supply source or a few key customers
Inability to generate sufficient revenue	Gradual disappearance of profitability

10   See, for example, Quach, Sara et al (2021). The experience of regret in small business failure: who's to blame? *European Journal of marketing*, 55(8), 2201-2238; Karikari, Amoa-Gyarteng and Shephare, Dhiwayo (2022). The Impact of Capital Structure on Profitability of Nascent Small and Medium Enterprises in Ghana, *Journal of Business and Economic Research*, 17(2), 275-291; Bingham, Christopher B. and McDonald, Rory M. (2022). Mastering Innovation's Toughest Trade-Offs, *MIT Sloan Management Review*, 63(4), 66-72.

Nascent entrepreneurial firms are born with a variety of shortcomings and obstacles that initially inhibit the ability for many of them to survive and grow. Not unlike newly born human beings, these fragile, vulnerable firms must survive an unfamiliar and challenging environment. As a consequence, the majority of such firms will be eventually forced out of the market and liquidated. It is therefore important for would-be entrepreneurs to understand the vulnerabilities of their ventures and exert the necessary efforts to ensure their strength and survival. The main challenges that face the newly born firms are briefly summarized below:

- Lack of sufficient capital for continuous operations.
- The focus of narrow geographic horizon of local or regional markets.
- Limited use of appropriate technology.
- Inadequate understanding of the market/sector/industry because of absence of research.
- Unsuitable product/service for consumers' needs.
- Inexperienced management.
- Scarcity of innovation.
- Lack of strategic direction for the firm.
- Inability to recruit the necessary technical and managerial talent.
- Inaccurate identification of consumer needs.
- Intense competition.

Undoubtedly, the efforts to establish and administer successful entrepreneurial companies are intimidating because of uncertainty and fear of failure that entrepreneurs encounter. Key venture startup requirements must be present to achieve business continuity and attain growth. For instance, critical resources must be assembled, market identified, customers served, and strategies crafted and deployed. In any case, the expanding influence of entrepreneurial and other small firms in the economy can briefly be attributed to four factors: (1) the increasing number of individuals who are willing to assume the risk to establish their own companies, (2) the growing demand for goods and services in the country, (3) the relative stability of the country's political and social systems, and (4) government support for small businesses via flexible regulations, grants, and loan guarantee.

Entrepreneurial Success: Guidelines for Entrepreneurs

As indicated earlier, most newly established business firms in the United States are squeezed out of the market in less than five years of their existence. Business failure represents a huge cost in terms of efforts, capital, and other resources to the entrepreneurs concerned and the national economy. So, what should the entrepreneur do to increase the probability of success of the business venture? Of course, there is no rule or formula for entrepreneurial success because success is subject to many influences some of which are beyond the control of the entrepreneur. There are, however, a few recommended moves that the entrepreneur can pursue prior to the founding of the venture and after its establishment, as outlined below:

- **Work on the Vision**. Ensure a realistic vision for the venture (i.e., the business concept). Refine it, if needed, to adapt to changes in the market or the industry.
- **Research the Market**. Conduct market research to verify short-term (one year) and intermediate-term (three years) demand for the venture's product or service.
- **Scrutinize the Business Model**. Study the business model (cost, revenue, and profit) with extra care to ensure the viability of the venture. The venture should be technically and economically viable to achieve success. "Technically" means that the product can by created and delivered with available machines, equipment, and other means of production. On the other hand, "economically" indicates that the product should be profitable within the foreseeable future.
- **Gauge Needed Resources**. Understand the time, efforts, technology, capital, and other resources required for the establishment and management of the venture.
- **Choose a Proper Legal Entity**. Decide on the initial legal form of the venture (e.g., sole proprietorship, corporation, etc.).

- **Define Strategy**. Plot the venture's grand strategy and functional strategies (e.g., marketing, finance, etc.) and incorporate the strategies in the business plan.
- **Examine the Competition**. Learn about major competitors, their products, prices, and market strategy.
- **Find Good People**. Seek to recruit qualified personnel for the company.
- **Rely on Experts for Advice**. Enlist the help of a business expert, consulting firm, or the SBA to review the business plan.
- **Respect and Delegate**. Manage the company in consultation with your management team.

Chapter Summary

This chapter presented an overall view of entrepreneurship, entrepreneurs, and entrepreneurial firms. Entrepreneurial firms are found in all economic sectors and industries including agriculture, healthcare, engineering, biotechnology, and consulting. The main task of entrepreneurs is to monitor, seek, analyze, take advantage of business opportunities and, in the process, create wealth for themselves and society. Opportunities come about because of demand for goods and services by consumers, government, business firms, and other nations.

Entrepreneurial firms, like their larger counterparts, can successfully exploit market opportunities with innovative goods and services. A business opportunity is an occasion which makes it possible for an entrepreneur to exploit something of value. Opportunities come about because of changes in economic, technological, and other external variables. Spending by consumers creates opportunities, so does spending by governments and organizations. Natural and man-made disasters play a role in the opportunity creation as well.

Entrepreneurs' decisions to take advantage of opportunities are influenced by several factors including expected profit and degree of risk involved. Entrepreneurship is governed by a host of factors such as government policy, availability of founding, workforce skills, and national attitude towards the business community. Many factors affect entrepreneurial success such as the entrepreneur's realistic vision, market knowledge, and the introduction of innovative goods and or services.

Entrepreneurship theories address the motivating factors for individuals to engage in entrepreneurial activity via the creation of business firms. Many theories emphasize the role of personality characteristics, resource availability, and existence of economic opportunities. Finally, the deployment of appropriate and affordable technology in entrepreneurial ventures is an important condition for success.

Chapter Questions

1. Explain the differences between small business owners and entrepreneurs.
2. Discuss the contributions of small firms to the nation's competitiveness.
3. Discuss the future of entrepreneurship in the United States.
4. Discuss the entrepreneurship ecosystem for high-technology industry in the United States.
5. Explain some of the entrepreneurship theories.

Chapter 2

Vision, the Product, the Market, and Competitive Advantage

"Plan for what it is difficult while it is easy, do what is great while it is small."

Sun Tzu

Learning Objectives:

- Appreciate the importance of business planning.
- Understand the process of planning.
- Know how to write a business plan.
- Learn about the business concept, business model, and venture's vision.

Careful planning is a sensible approach in the business world for making strategic decisions that have far reaching consequences for the business enterprise. Planning has many benefits. For instance, it maximizes the anticipated rewards of venture decisions and minimizes their costs. Planning is needed even for the establishment of a smallest business venture such as a "mom-and-pop" business with one or two employees. The consequence of good planning in this case, for example, is to help the owner avoid unnecessary loss of invested funds and efforts.

Business Concept, Business Model, and the Business Plan

The entrepreneurial process begins with the entrepreneur's determination of the concept for the business venture. This includes deciding on its nature, its purpose, its industry, its target market, and its target customers. To illustrate, let's assume that a would-be entrepreneur defines her business concept by indicating that she is thinking to establish a company in the software industry to develop and sell a software package to assist students summarize lengthy book chapters or other materials into several short statements for easy understanding and recollection. In this example, the would-be entrepreneur has identified the product, the sector or industry, target customers, and the target market.

Defining a good business concept requires knowledge of the concept's elements (e.g., the product, the market, etc.). This knowledge can be acquired either prior to the formation of the business concept or after defining it. Quite often, the business concept is related to the entrepreneur's overall vision (i.e., visualization of the future). For instance, an entrepreneur might have a vision to create a group of business firms. Entrepreneurs have also unique vision (i.e., future destination) for each business firm they establish. On the other hand, the business model refers to the venture's future cost, revenue, and profit. The business model requires the development of financial profit and loss statements and balance sheets. These statements are incorporated into the venture's business plan. What is a Business Plan?

Planning is defined as a description of the future one envisions for a business venture including what one intends to do and how she plans to do it. However, a business plan is a document that provides background and financial information about the company, outlines the main goals for the business, and describes how the entrepreneur expects to reach them (Neck et al, 2018, pp. 203 and 225). Put differently, the plan for the venture can be envisioned as a drawing or chart designed by the entrepreneur to accomplish future tasks for the intended venture. The plan is also referred to as a list of "to do" activities. Many benefits can be derived for writing a realistic business plan including the following (e.g., Delmar and Scott, 2003;

Liao and Gartner, 2007/2008; Long et al, 2016; Ya-long et at, 2018):

- To introduce the venture to interested parties (e.g., venture capitalists, suppliers, etc.)
- To assist in generating funds, finding partnership, or making strategic alliances.
- To guide the entrepreneur during the various stages of venture creation.
- To facilitate internal communication with employees and external contacts with suppliers, customers, government agencies, and so on.
- To press the entrepreneur to devise marketing and sales strategies.
- To help the entrepreneur focus on business opportunities.
- To assist the entrepreneur in validating her idea about the business venture.

A well-devised business plan offers many benefits to entrepreneurs and other business owners including the following:

- It is a document that illustrates the venture's viability to future investors.
- It is an orderly method for summarizing, listing, and prioritizing key business activities.
- It paves the way for setting systems or procedures to monitor and control activities to attain better organizational performance.
- It provides the basis for the venture's strategy formulation and execution in functional areas such as sales, finance, logistics, and quality control.
- It sets the direction for the venture's growth and competitive advantage.
- It guides entrepreneurs to estimate future resource needs (e.g., managers, technical skills, technology, etc.).
- It is a communication channel with constituencies.

The contents of business plans vary from venture to venture, from industry to industry, and from market to market. Specific factors that influence the extent of the plan include (i) the size of the venture in terms of employment, (ii) the nature of the product or service to be offered, (iii) the required initial funding amount, (iv) target customers,

(v) the market structure (e.g., perfect competition, duopoly, etc.), and (vi) target market (e.g., local, national, international). The business plan generally includes the following tasks:

- Introduce the venture by indicating its name, its address, nature of the business, funding needs, and confidentiality statement.
- Create the executive summary.
- Explain the venture's value proposition. That is, the value that the venture will deliver to customers, the kind of the problem that venture tries to solve, and the features of the product or service.
- Determine the vision for the venture, that is, its nature, future direction, and destination.
- Construct the venture's business model about cost, revenue, and future.
- Formulate the venture's mission, key goals, and objectives.
- Demonstrate the venture's competitive advantage and its uniqueness.
- Define the nature of product (i.e., goods or services).
- Identify the target market (e.g., local, national, etc.), the target customers, the sector, and the industry.
- Indicate the main product channels of distribution.
- Provide a two-year assessment of cost, revenue, and profit.
- Estimate capital and other resources needed for the venture.
- Construct the organizational structure (i.e., the venture's skeleton).
- Declare the legal form of the company (e.g., partnership, corporation, etc.).

An example for business plan creation, Strategyzer.com proposes a so-called "business model canvas" which is an approach to step-by-step business planning in which the entrepreneur lists all key aspects related to the venture. The model can assist in developing a well-thought business plan. The example below illustrates the main components of the business plan suggested by this approach for a T-shirt manufacturing company:

- Value proposition (e.g., trendy T-shirts for kids, eco-friendly material, original design).

- Main partners (e.g., suppliers, artists, and designers).
- Core activities (e.g., managing employees, inventory, sales).
- Customer relationship (e.g., social media, merchandise promotion).
- Market segmentation (e.g., fashion conscious parents, trendy kinds).
- Major resources (e.g., store location, inventory, salespeople).
- Distribution channels (e.g., Internet, brick stores).
- Cost structure (e.g., employees, artists, rent, sales, and marketing).
- Revenue Structure (e.g., sales, interest on deposits).

Business Plan Software

Entrepreneurial and other small and mid-sized companies have during the past decade introduced to the market business planning software packages that would-be entrepreneurs need to know. Essentially, the software can be classified into two categories: (i) software designed for writing the business plan, and (ii) software intended to help the management of the business enterprise to conduct certain organizational functions in areas such as business strategy, production, project management, and financial planning. The list includes the following software products: *LivePlan, IdeaBody, Enloop, GoSmallBiz, Bizplan, ClearPoint Strategy, ClickUp, AchieveIt, SmartSheet,* and *QuickBooks Online.*

The Face-to-Face Interview

As the entrepreneur's business plan is initially accepted by a potential investor such as an angel investor, a brief face-to-face meeting is usually arranged for the entrepreneur to explain various aspects of the proposed venture. The more prominent topics that will be addressed concern the venture's management approach, plans for marketing and sales, and the venture's profitability, as briefly highlighted below:

- Management: The entrepreneurial management team represents the "engine" of the venture. It is the power that determines the venture's destination, its competitive advantage, and its long-term growth success. This requires the team be ready to demonstrates its managerial skills and other talents via documents submission, testimonies, and other necessary means.

- Marketing and Sales: It is well-known in the business community that marketing-driven companies are usually high-growth companies. As is the case with the venture's leadership, the marketing and sales team should possess the skills and expertise needed to move products or services across different regional, national, and international markets. Key questions that are often asked are: Is the team aware of the overall market size and expected growth rate? Are the prices for products or services market-competitive in view of market conditions? Is the team sufficiently motivated for the task ahead? Is it familiar with competing products or services?

- Financial Analysis: Prospective investors are very much interested in the analysis of startups' financials including the income statement, cash flow statement, and the balance sheet for the foreseeable two to three years. Such analysis will shed light on venture's expected revenue, cost, and profit, in addition to learning its assets and liabilities. The result will be to gauge the venture's financial worthiness and its ability to generate earnings.

The Venture's Business Plan and Competitive Advantage

Competitive advantage is generally defined as an edge that distinguishes a venture from other companies in the same line of business, sector, and industry. The business plan, as an indispensable tool by which to entice potential investors, should demonstrate the venture's long-term viability as the marketplace is full of competing goods and services as well as product substitutes. Fledgling entrepreneurs needs to be cognizant of the fact that competition takes place in different forms, including price, quality, shape, weight, color, convenience, availability, and trademark. As such, companies can achieve competitive advantage in a variety of ways, including through the following:

- Achievable business strategy (e.g., vision, goals)

- Patents
- Attractiveness of the product (a good or service)
- Technology competency
- Human skills competency (e.g., management team, technical, etc.)
- Physical assets (e.g., real estate, equipment, etc.)
- Customer service
- Speed of delivery
- Company reputation
- Availability of sufficient financial resources
- Networks (e.g., suppliers, customers, etc.).

Executive Summary: An Example

Wise Business Plans (wisebusinessplans.com) has made available to the public detailed business plans for different ventures in various industries. Below is an abbreviated and edited example of an executive summary for one of the very small (i.e., micro) ventures called Thiktand:

Thinktank is a business service provider based in Miami, Florida. Founded by Mrs. Cindy Smith, It will offer a variety of services including postal, shipping, faxing and copying to the local residents. The local area has been in dire need of a service of this type for some time and Thinktank plans to adequately serve them. The founder projects needing 100K for the business venture with repayment being made out of the profits. The marketing will be done through a variety of mediums including the Internet, mass media, print and networking. Internet efforts will center on the creation of a user-friendly website that clearly list all of the core services that will be offered. The website will be developed using the latest in online technologies including SEO (Search Engine Optimization) which will allow for a much higher ranking in popular search engines like Yahoo.com and Google.com to name a few. In addition to the home website, plans also call for the creation of a strong social media presence using Facebook.com and Twitter.com. Thinktank marketing model will be mass media driven by commercials appearing on ABC as well as professional networking done through local chambers of commerce and business networking groups and affiliates. The financials for the company are quite promising and bode well for future expansion into other sectors of the region and service areas. The overhead costs are moderate and that salaries are also projected to be moderate as the founder does not project adding additional employees during the initial stages of market entry. Marketing and operations expenditures will be the bulk of the expenses during each of the projected years.

Upon reading the above executive summary, what do you think should also be included to make the proposed venture more appealing for funding?

Chapter Summary

Entrepreneurs in search of venture funding must prepare a detailed business plan. The plan is a document that serves as a tool to introduce the business venture to selected outsiders, usually angel investors and venture capitalists. The investor review process begins with "due diligence" in which the plan is subjected, after the initial acceptance review, to a thorough study to ascertain the likelihood for success and the venture being investment worthy.

The plan also provides a basis for evaluating whether or not investors will be able to recoup their investment with attractive financial returns. In preparing the document, the entrepreneur should seek the help of a business consultant familiar with the economic conditions of the market, sector, and industry. The plan's broad outline should include the vision for the venture, its purpose, its competitive advantage, market analysis, sales forecasting, and resource requirements.

There are many advantages for a well-designed and well-researched business plan including increased probability for external financing, better strategic initiatives, and enhanced company performance. In the face-to-face interview, the entrepreneur must be able to demonstrate in a relatively short period of time the viability of the proposed venture and its future success.

Chapter Questions

1. What is a business plan?
2. Explain the reasons for the entrepreneur to develop a business plan.
3. What is the main difference between the business concept and business model?
4. What are the five most important components of a business plan?
5. How would you go about developing your own business plan for a business consulting venture?

Chapter 3

The Search for Venture Financing

"Money is important, but how much do you need?"

N. Ganeshan

Learning Objectives:

- Understand the need for venture financing.
- Discuss the main sources of financing.
- Grasp the criteria of financing.
- Evaluate financing offers.

It is common knowledge that invested capital (money, funds, cash) is the most important ingredient for establishing, managing, and growing a business enterprise including startup ventures. Capital is needed to pay employees, suppliers, insurance, rent, taxes, and other individuals and organizations. Insufficient or lack of capital can eventually force the enterprise to exit the market or render the efforts to launch the venture become unsuccessful.

Many clever entrepreneurs come up with creative venture ideas to offer the market innovative goods or services. However, the initial obstacle they face is acquiring the necessary funds for the startup venture. Moreover, they may lack the knowledge of how much invested capital they need during the first or subsequent years of the venture's operations. This chapter addresses sources of finance that may be available to entrepreneurs to enable them to launch a business venture.

Sources of Venture Funding

The U.S. economy, unlike many other economies, is highly receptive and encouraging to entrepreneurial activity and the private sector. Newly established innovative ventures receive billions of dollars in venture financing annually. For example, Table 1 below shows the funding that some companies received according to the 2022 CNBC disruptors 50:

Table 1

CNBC Disruptors 50

Company	Industry/Sector	Funding ($ millions)
Flexport	Logistics	2,200
Brex	Fintch	1,200
Discord	Media	1,100
Canva	Enterprise technology	560
Guide Education	Education	379
Truepill	Healthcare	257
Arctic Wolf	Cybersecurity	498

Source: www.cnbc.com, May 17, 2022.

Sources of entrepreneurial and small business funding can be classified into two main categories, as indicated below:

Informal sources. These include:

Personal savings. Having sufficient savings for a startup venture is the best first step in entrepreneurial activities especially for a relatively small business. Data show, however, that only five percent of the U.S. population have some amount of savings, while the rest of the population are largely in debt. In the absence or inadequacy of personal savings, the entrepreneur can resort to other informal sources such as the use of credit cards or selling one's personal property.

Borrowing from family members, relatives, or friends. This approach to borrowing can yield some amounts of money, though modest and likely to be insufficient to create an ambitious venture.

In additional to (or lack of) informal funding, entrepreneurs with well-developed business plans can seek formal sources to fund the venture, as discussed below.

Formal sources. Entrepreneurs or small business owners can pursue financing from different formal sources. The most notable sources are:

Commercial Banks. Banks in the United States are likely willing to consider venture loan applications within certain funding limits and other criteria established by each funding institution. In general, the criteria used to evaluate a loan application involve (i) the applicant's credit rating, (ii) income level, (iii) sources of income, (iv) financial and other assets, (v) education and experience, (vi) purpose of the loan, and (vii) and the venture's viability and its expected return.

Bank borrowing, however, entails in many instances a high rate of interest and may levy a heavy financial burden on entrepreneurs or small business owners. Clearly, if borrowing is to be rewarding, the borrowed money should generate a return on investment that exceeds the original loan plus the interest.

SBA and NSF. The U.S. Small Business Administration (SBA) has created a program called SBA-guaranteed loans whereby entrepreneurs are matched with prospective banks for borrowing purposes. This program involves four steps according to the SBA: (i) the applicant is to contact the agency to answer a few personal questions about the nature of the venture and its goals, (ii) getting matched with potential lenders upon approval, (iii) applicant review of terms and conditions of the loan, and (iv) loan application if approved.

On the other hand, the U.S National Science Foundation (seedfund. nsf.gov) offers at least $2 million in the form of seed money grant for entrepreneurial companies and others for early-stage product development.

Angel investors. Angel investors have become an important source of financing especially for innovative ventures. Angel investors are normally wealthy individuals many of whom are retired executives and are willing to (i) offer funds as seed money and for startup venture operations, (ii) provide managerial and technical support to entrepreneurs, and (iii) assist entrepreneurs to expand their business, managerial, and technical networks. Angel investors, as capital suppliers, set their own criteria to evaluate potential success and sustainability of entrepreneurial ventures. Angel investors financing in the United States has been growing in recent years as more groups of investors have joined forces. An example of angel investors is the New York Angels (www.newyorkangels.com). Members of this group are willing to invest between $100,000 and $1,500,000 per round of capital raise. The ventures' investment criteria of this group include the following factors:

- Targe market of the company, its intended market size, and the market growth rate.
- A comprehensive business plan that shows proven concept behind the product or technology as well as identification of potential competitors.
- The venture's management team.
- Financial projection, sales strategy, and profit potential.
- Exit strategy that yield at least ten times the angels' initial investment.

Venture Capitalists. Venture capitalists (VCs) are individual investors, group of investors, or investment companies that provide capital to potentially high-growth, innovative business ventures. VCs are equity investors who typically seek an equity stake in the ventures they finance. As is the case with many angel investors, venture capitalists support startups in a variety of ways.

For example, in addition to participating in startups financing, they tend to play an active role to ensure the survival and long-term progress of the ventures concerned. They assist in the deployment of technology, employment of critical expertise, and recommendation of strategic initiatives (e.g., Karimkhani, Mehrdad et al, 2022). As is the case with other official lenders, VCs utilize their own lending criteria to evaluate the merit (or demerit) of business plans which may include the following factors:

- Personality attributes of the entrepreneur (e.g., integrity, track record, skills, experience, ability to react to business risk).
- The venture's product or service (e.g., market acceptance, legal protection, potential market growth, market size).
- The venture's leadership team (e.g., managerial, marketing, and technical skills).
- The venture's financial prospects (e.g., revenue, return on investment, profitability).
- The economic environment (e.g., economic growth, consumer spending, government spending).
- The legal environment (e.g., small business regulations, tax rates, institutional support for entrepreneurial companies).

Financing via the Internet (crowdfunding). In recent years, the Internet has increasingly become a significant platform for electronic commerce (e-commerce) whereby goods and services are bought and sold. In addition, the Internet has made it possible for the wide spread of social media and its adoption by platforms such as Facebook, WhatsApp, and LinkedIn. Entrepreneurs and other small business owners can utilize the Internet and social media to raise money by inviting the public to participate in startups ventures. This approach to startup funding is often called "crowdfunding" whereby a public investor gains a share in proportion to their contribution in the newly established company.

Grants. Young business ventures with promising product, service, or technology should search for available grants offered by U.S. government agencies and corporations such as the Department of Defense, National

Aeronautics and Space Administration (NASA), National Institute of Health, and FedEx Small Business Grants Contest. Unlike loans, grants are "free" money normally intended to support fledgling entrepreneurs in their entrepreneurial projects. Grants are highly competitive sources of funds. Grant proposals, therefore, need to be well-thought of, well-researched, and well-written, as is the case with all funding requests.

General Funding Guidelines

A doable venture idea is a starting point for venture creation. Good business ideas are always in need for funding to be translated into real-world business enterprise. How should an entrepreneur who seeks funding prepare for a meeting with VCs or other potential investors for venture funding? Prospective investors and lenders are keen to ensure they will receive back their original investment (or loan) plus the expected financial return. As such, they expect the entrepreneur to introduce the business venture and cover the following:

- The entrepreneur's business experience, education, risk tolerance, skills, and vision. Early in the meeting, the entrepreneur is typically given the opportunity to make the pitch, a short, concise statement about the entrepreneur, the venture, the amount of needed funding, and the purpose of funding.
- Management team industry experience, integrity, and skills.
- The venture's product or service, goals, market research, target customers, scope of the market, anticipated market growth, major competitors, technology to be deployed, and the venture's sources of competitive advantage.
- Amount of funds needed, uses of funds, other sources of funds, and cost of doing business.
- Anticipated annual revenue and profit in the short-and intermediate term.

Chapter Summary

Entrepreneurs and would-be entrepreneurs like the rest of society can generate creative ideas and act upon them. In the business world, however, ideas for startup ventures must pass the test of simultaneously being technically feasible (i.e., can be implemented from a technological point of view) and economically feasible (i.e., can generate a stream of profits). There are several sources of venture funding in the United States including family members and friends, the public, banks, angel investors, venture capitalists, and grants. The entrepreneur's qualifications along with her team and the quality and realism of the startup venture are important ingredients for securing financing. Seeking external funds demands that the entrepreneur be ready to defend her vision and capability for the startup venture in front of potential investors by answering a variety of questions and providing supporting evidence.

Chapter Questions

1. Are there differences between angel investors and venture capitalists in terms of venture financing criteria?
2. Discuss the sources of venture financing.
3. What would be your "pitch" for your own startup business in the industry of your choice?
4. Discuss the importance of funding to the business enterprise.
5. What is the role of SBA in entrepreneurial and small business lending?

Chapter 4

Bird's -Eye View of Management and the Business Enterprise

"Management is, above all, a practice where art, science, and craft meet."

Henry Mintzberg

Learning Objectives:

- Grasp the meaning of management.
- Know about managerial responsibilities.
- Master management principles
- Realize the need for motivating employees.

We begin by explaining the terms "management" and the "business enterprise." Management implies two distinct meanings. First, it refers to a body of knowledge – a discipline – that consists of principles, theories, techniques, and strategies. As a discipline, management has been taught within the broader field of business administration in colleges and universities in the United States and other countries. Second, management is also viewed in the business community to refer to officially appointed or an elected group of people at the top and middle leadership echelon of the enterprise entrusted to guide it to profitability and competitiveness. The emphasis in this book is on management as a discipline.

On the other hand, the term "business enterprise" refers to a legal entity established primarily for-profit purposes. Management and the business enterprise are invariably linked to each other because no enterprise, however small, can exist without having its own management to administer its operations and lead it to success. People create businesses to own, manage, grow, profit from and, in the process, contribute to society's needs and desires for quality, affordable goods and services.

The business enterprise is then born to perform certain functions, cultivate economic opportunities, reward its owners and employees, and promote society's aspiration. As the innovative enterprise grows, so does its appetite to plow greater opportunities and seek to conquer new markets. As the enterprise grows, the tasks and responsibilities of its management expand and become more challenging.

The Practice and Purpose of Management

Management is a complex practice especially within large organizations. It involves many facets, includes many functions, and takes place in a dynamic environment. Specialists have attempted over the years to summarize the meaning of management in a concise statement of definitions. For example, management is often defined as a process of planning, organizing, leading, and controlling human and other scarce resources of the organization to achieve desired goals effectively and efficiently (e.g., Hatten, 2020; Jones and George, 2014).

This traditional definition of management highlights the scope and main duties of managers, but it represents a broad statement of overall managerial activities. It doesn't address, for instance, specific managerial activities such as marketing or quality control. Second, the definition assumes that all managers and executives in the organization are equally responsible to perform the four tasks referred to above. For these and other reasons, some specialists prefer to define the concept of management as simply "getting things done."

In any case, the four tasks of planning, organizing, leading, and controlling are indeed key tasks of middle and top management in the organization.

Management in the business world constitutes the growth engine of the enterprise. It is the mechanism that creates and carries out the vision, mission, direction, and strategies of the enterprise. Management creates purpose, hope, and value for the enterprise, and brings about order, discipline, motivation, systems, rewards, and policies. In many enterprises, especially mid-sized and large firms, managerial levels are generally grouped into three categories:

- First-line management (or supervisors).
- Middle-management (e.g., units/sections/departments managers).
- Top management (e.g., Chief executive officers, vice presidents, division chiefs)

Some large firms such as multinational organizations have five or more managerial levels, depending on the complexity and relative size of their operations, nature of goods or services they offer, and the extent of their business globalization. In successful enterprises, the responsibilities of the different levels of management (also called tasks, functions, or duties) are congruent and aligned with each other to attain the enterprise desired goals and objectives.

The management makeup in the early years of a newly established startup venture is often simple and consists of one managerial layer, that is, the entrepreneur along with a few employees, if any. This form of organizational structure is called flat because it consists of one level of management. The structure becomes more complex by moving towards multiple managerial layers as the entrepreneurial company succeeds and grows over time. As the newly founded startup venture lacks sufficient financial resources, it should not attempt in its early stage of operations to recruit full-time employees unless they are urgently needed. Many of the venture's activities can be outsourced for quality work at reasonable prices.

Management Principles

It is common in modern organizations today for managers to be responsible for such functions as leading, planning, organizing, recruiting, training, evaluating, and controlling. Effective administration of people, technology, and other critical resources is a serious managerial responsibility that requires vision, wisdom, and guiding principles. Management discipline offers enduring tenets that help create orderly workplace relations, better resource allocation, and sensible distribution of authority and decision-making in the enterprise. Some of the management principles are borrowed from military practices while others are adopted from the fields of economics, sociology, and psychology. Still other principles have emerged as a result of research findings as well as from successful managerial experiences. The principles are interrelated and intertwined, and in their totality should be viewed as guidelines for successful managerial practices within organizations. As alluded to earlier, managing scarce resources should be driven by thoughtful, calculating, and wise decisions and not forced upon the organization by arbitrary or aimless actions. The following principles are among the most widely followed principles in well-managed firms (see for example, Volkema and Kapoutsis, 2016; Witzel, 2002; Fuller, 2022; Islam, 2022).

Chain of Command (Scalar Chain). This principle stipulates that business firms are governed by the authority of managerial hierarchy in which individuals at lower managerial levels (or positions) are required to report directly to higher managerial levels, and that the chain of command extends to reach vice presidents, the chief executive officer, and the board of directors.

Violation of this fundamental principle can cause chaos and disruption within the workplace for the obvious reason that confusion may result as employees will not know who is in charge for important decision-making. Executive managers – especially those within entrepreneurial companies – need to inform employees clearly as to who they need to report to or receive instructions or directives from. Employees should not be left to their own assumptions or hunches.

Span of Control. According to this principle a limit should be imposed on the number of subordinates reporting to a manager or supervisor. The logic is that a typical manager or supervisor has limited physical and mental energy in any given day, and if many employees report to the individual, then she will tend to become less effective or efficient and may make wrong decisions. The principle does not set a specific level of subordinates because the limit differs from job to job and from industry to industry. The following are factors that should be taken into consideration in setting the limit for the span of control:

- The nature of the job performed. (e.g., mental versus physical, routine versus scientific). For example, a manger in a janitorial firm can handle more janitors – because of their simple tasks - than a manger in a scientific research institution whose unit is entrusted with research activities.
- Employees' education, skills, and experience.
- The firm's size and its economic sector of operations.
- The manager's or supervisor's experience, job knowledge, and skills.

As the entrepreneurial enterprise grows in terms of employment over time, its leadership needs to observe the impact of its span of control, in various organizational levels, on its cost structure and profitability to take the necessary decisions, if needed, to rectify the situation.

Unity of Command. According to unity of command there should be one leader (i.e., boss) assigned to manage a group of employees who perform identical or similar functions in the organization. The existence of two or more leaders to directly lead the same group of employees causes instability because of possibly conflicting instructions or directives from the leaders.

Authority and Responsibility Parity. This principle specifies that the responsibility delegated to an employee, regardless of the employee's position within the organization, should be accompanied with an equivalent degree of authority. In fact, assigning job accountability to employees without the proper authority can jeopardize the effective workplace and can create undesirable ramifications such as resentment or job dissatisfaction.

Division of Labor. Division of labor has been widely utilized by business firms, government agencies, and academic institutions. Division of labor and specialization occur when top management divides organization's functions (e.g., marketing, production, accounting) into appropriate components such as units, departments, and divisions, and assigns each function to well-trained, specialized employees. The division of organizational functions into different groups is normally called departmentalization. The main benefit of departmentalization is to increase an organization's productivity and output.

It is worthwhile to point out at this juncture that entrepreneurs should be aware of other managerial and organizational guidelines and practices that have emerged and gained traction over the years including:

- *Continuous improvement*: Organizational progress should be measured by higher standards of performance in quality, cost, productivity, and so on.
- *Structure and Strategy*: The firm's structure is to accommodate its strategies. The implication for entrepreneurs, for example, is that they need first to craft the strategy for the venture (e.g., the kind of output, vision, goals) prior to creating the venture itself.
- *Innovation*: In a global environment of cut-throat competition, scientific advances, and emerging technologies, the name of the game is innovation. Innovation becomes an indispensable activity for the firm that enables it to survive and grow.

Leadership Responsibilities

Entrepreneurs ought to understand their responsibilities and functions within the business venture. Key responsibilities of visionary individuals at the top of the managerial echelon in well-managed business firms revolve around the effective and efficient accomplishment of the organization's main activities. The individuals concerned include the Chief Executive Officer (CEO), vice presidents, division chiefs, and directors. The activities are related to the firm's functional areas such as marketing and finance as well as managerial functions such as planning and controlling. The activities that constitute the bulk of the functions are summarized below:

- Determine the vision (long-term strategic direction) of the enterprise and ensure its attainment. Although the crafting of the firm's vision is a primary function of the CEO, senior managers often play a key role in shaping it.
- Recognize business opportunities for the firm such as the introduction of new products or services, entering new markets, forging strategic alliances, adopting new technology, and deploying diversification strategies.
- Oversee the formulation of the firm's strategic and functional plans and ensure the availability of the necessary resources for their effective implementation.
- Build the firm's core and distinctive competencies with emphasis on innovation, organizational performance, and the development of company-wide critical skills.
- Promote the firm's relations with its constituencies such as clients, communities, governmental agencies, vendors, and employees. Utilize the social media including platforms such as YouTube to reach a world-wide audience.
- Resolve major internal conflicts, boost morale, reward innovation efforts, and appreciate initiatives and excellence.
- Emphasize the firm's core values (i.e., company culture), corporate citizenship, and ethical business practices, and customer service.
- Ensure smooth functioning of the firm by delegating authority to subordinates and assessing their performance.
- Deploy appropriate technology, conduct market research, employ competent workforce, and seek new business ideas.
- Decide on sources and uses of capital for the firm's short-, intermediate-, and long-term.
- Achieve sustainable growth and a competitive advantage for the firm.

Typically, the CEO accomplishes her responsibilities in cooperation with, and support of, senior executives of the enterprise, whose functions are also to administer middle managers and ensure the proper functioning of their units and divisions as well as the organization as a whole. The responsibilities of the CEO are invariably associated with extensive official meetings in and outside the enterprise. The responsibilities of entrepreneurs in newly established entrepreneurial ventures are very much the same as the CEO's in, for instance, mid-sized firms except that these firms are normally larger and richer in resources and scope of operations. On the other hand, the main tasks of middle management in many firms is to ensure the implementation of the organization's grand strategy as well as the functional strategies of their respective areas of operations such as sales, accounting, finance, logistics, and customer retention. Specifically, the primary responsibilities of middle-management include the following:

- Developing strategies for their units, departments, and divisions as well as ensuring their effective implementation.
- Supervising the preparation of annual budgets of their respective domain of operations.
- Deciding on recruitment and professional development of the workforce within their functional areas of responsibility.
- Ensuring efficient allocation of resources.
- Maintaining contacts with customers, suppliers, managers, and other business parties.
- Administering the overall operations of their functional areas.

The main responsibilities of first-line management or supervisors include the following:

- Supervising day-to-day activities of employees within the designated area of the supervisor.
- Developing operational (i.e., daily) plans for the designated units of operations.
- Attending the unit and company scheduled meetings.
- Providing daily, weekly, or monthly reports to higher management concerning their activities, needs, and

achievements.

- Requesting supplies, equipment, software, and other needs for the unit.
- Training, managing, and evaluating the performance of subordinates.
- Participating in professional development activities (e.g., workshops, seminars).
- Contacting suppliers, customers, and organizations as directed by a higher-level manager.
- Ensuring a proper work environment for subordinates.

Decisions at the Top

The main role of senior management in many organizations is to (i) make strategic decisions to meet business goals, (ii) monitor the outcomes of the decisions, (iii) move the organization forward, and (iv) attain sustainable growth of the firm. The decisions are called strategic because of their importance to the entire enterprise. The decisions are usually guided by:

- The Chief executive officer's vision for the firm.
- Market research, the industry environment, and the health of the economy.
- Personal experience and wisdom, consultations, and expected strategic moves by major rival firms.
- Resource availability.
- Management appetite for risk-taking.
- Industry factors such as the economic and competitive environment.

Compared to routine decisions (e.g., day-to-day decisions), strategic decisions extend to include long-term planning for:

- The introduction of new or improved products.
- Moves to reach (or penetrate further into) national and/or global markets.
- Adoption of appropriate technology for the firm.
- Diversification into new business and products. Acquisition of

critical resources such as technical and managerial talents to enhance the firm's innovation efforts and competitive advantage.

- Forging strategic alliances with suppliers, customers, and other firms.

In recent years, a variety of advanced statistical analysis (e.g., data analytics, regression analysis, econometrics) embodied in software programs along with the deployment of high-speed computers are deployed to assist in long-and-intermediate panning and decision-making. Undoubtedly, the firm's competitive analysis influences final decisions for dealing with major problems or issues that encounter the business enterprise. In any event, strategic decisions are normally aimed at addressing two categories of organizational issues, as indicated below:

- To tackle short-or immediate-term important issues such as (i) internal or external disasters facing the firm, (ii) initiating organizational restructuring, (iii) encountering large decline in demand.
- To strengthen the enterprise for the long-term, for example, because of (i) anticipation of substantial increase in demand, (ii) planning for new markets penetration, (iii) contemplating joint ventures, or (iv) overhauling the technological base of the enterprise.

The cumulative effect of strategic decisions is to position the firm in the marketplace in such a way as to achieve sustainable competitive advantage, an advantage that enables it to reap market opportunities and enjoy economic benefits in the long-term. This outcome is the ultimate goal of the firm's growth-oriented strategies.

Strategizing

A business enterprise must be modeled to reach its desired destination, that is, to attain the vision articulated by its managerial leadership. Strategizing (also called the strategic management process or the strategic management model) is the process by which leadership creates strategic plans that help the enterprise to arrive at desired outcomes. Strategizing involves the following steps:

- Analyzing the firm's external situation with emphasis on its industry environment to identify economic opportunities as well as threats.
- Assessing the firm's internal situation to be aware of strengths and weaknesses.
- Developing the firm's Strengths, Weaknesses, Opportunity, and Threat (SWOT) profile.
- Using the SWOT analysis to create alternative business strategies (or strategic initiatives).
- Utilizing value judgment, experience, and quantitative methods to formulate and evaluate best possible strategies.

Strategizing requires crafting the firm's vision and developing its mission, major goals, and specific steps (called objectives) to help achieve desired goals. A growing mid-sized or large firm can deploy any number of strategies during its lifetime. Strategies include diversification, integration, differentiation, and joint ventures. As the firm grows, it tends to extend its market reach to include the international market and gradually becomes a Multi-National Corporation (MNC). In general, firms tend to espouse specific strategies as they are guided by certain considerations, including:

- Appropriateness of the strategy in view of the firm's vision and goals.
- Relevance of the strategy to the industry's environment.
- Pertinence of the strategy to the firm's own resources and capabilities.
- Expected risks that may result from implanting the desired strategy.
- Suitability of the strategy in view of external forces such as the health of the economy, consumer demand, and government regulations.
- Expected benefits derived from strategy execution, especially in terms of improving (or maintaining) the firm's competitive advantage.
- Anticipated return on invested capital as a result of strategy implementation in the intermediate-and long-term.

Managing Employees' Motivation

A business enterprise is more than just the name it carries. It is also more than a collection of employees, managers, executives, technology, and other human and physical resources. The business enterprise should be viewed as a purposeful gathering of human beings with souls, spirits, and aspirations assisted by leadership, technology, systems, and policies with the intention of offering goods and services at competitive quality and price. Realizing that the firm is more than just inputs, processes, and outputs will lead its management to value the efforts of employees and motivate them to reach their full potential and, thus, boost further their contributions.

Research on workforce motivation is extensive. For example, the contributions of renowned scholars such as Abraham Maslow (hierarchy of needs theory), Victor H. Vroom (Vroom expectancy theory) Douglas McGregor (theory X and theory Y), Frederic Herzberg (hygiene factors and motivators) just to mention a few have advanced our knowledge about human beings and the factors that influence employees' motivation, productivity, and organizational loyalty. In brief, the essence of many well-researched motivation theories is that the workforce is the pillar of innovation and growth in organizations and, as such, should be guided, nurtured, and motivated. More specifically, key elements of influential theories are summarized below:

- Motivation is an issue of importance to both employees and the business firm. Senior management, therefore, ought to understand the ever-changing motivational factors affecting modern organizations and positively respond to them. The factors include family responsibility, lifestyle, COVID -19, and alternative employment.
- Most employees in the new environment of diversity and inclusion are believed to be willing to exert extra efforts in the workplace and would certainly respond actively for being appreciated and motivated.
- Employees who feel they are fairly treated and valued by management tend to be more productive than those who feel

ignored or unfairly treated.

Factors that affect workforce motivation are many including the firm's policies and decisions about the following:

- Professional development of employees.
- Job enrichment and advancement.
- Managerial leadership opportunities for employees.
- Fairness in the treatment of employees.
- A workplace that is free from physical and emotional harm or abuse.

In the aftermath of the COVID-19 pandemic, an increasing number of employees are also pursuing hybrid work assignments and employment in which they are allowed to perform their duties in the confine of the firm's office as well as remotely. Hybrid work arrangements or purely remote work have become a key motivational factor, especially to attract skilled individuals.

Chapter Summary

Management is an intriguing subject, discipline, and practice. It is universal in scope and influence. The business enterprise must be managed wisely to properly achieve its mission, vision, and strategic goals. As members of organizations, small or large, people will be managed by others, manage others, or both. There is no escape from the reach and power of management. Managers at different levels of the enterprise are generally involved in planning, coordinating, and executing a range of tasks as well as reviewing and organizing activities. Deciding on the long-term direction of the enterprise and ensuring the sufficiency of its success are the ultimate functions of the firm's CEO and her team of senior executives.

Managers must understand the importance of management principles such as unity of command. Motivating employees with the help of sensible policies and decisions is a responsibility of top management. There is an extensive body of research that shows evidence of the importance of motivation to improve employees' commitment, productivity, and loyalty to the organization. For example, Pandzic and Hadziahmetovic (2022) believe that financial and non-financial rewards play essential roles in (i) motivating employees, (ii) strengthening their bonds with the organization, and (iii) increasing their workplace engagement. On the other hand, Della-Giustina et al (2022) assert that improving employees' safety in the workplace and paying attention to their health conditions are motivational factors that lead to increased productivity and boosting of morale.

Chapter Questions

1. What is management?
2. What is the role of management in society?
3. How many managerial levels is optimal for a small bank? Explain.
4. What should be the qualifications of individuals at middle management? Discuss.
5. Discuss how to best motivate lazy employees.

Chapter 5

The Private Sector and the Business Enterprise

"Good business leaders create a vision, articulate the vision, passionately own the vision, and relentlessly drive it to completion."

Jack Welsh

Learning Objectives:

- Recognize the purpose of the private sector.
- Review the environmental forces impacting the firm.
- Appreciate the importance of organizational structure.
- Learn about the purpose of the business enterprise.

The U.S. economy is a free market system in which prices of goods and services including gold, petroleum, and currencies, are determined by market forces, that is, by supply and demand. The role of government is to ensure an orderly functioning of the market via the enforcement of laws, regulations, and other legal means.

Functions of the Private Sector

The U.S. private sector is the largest in the world and represents the lion's share of the national economy. It's created, owned, and managed by individuals and business firms. The sector includes a variety of small, mid-sized, and large enterprises that operate in a wide range of productive activities including agricultural, industrial, and service industries. The operations of many firms extend beyond the country's border to embrace international markets in Africa, the middle East, Asia, Europe, and Latin America.

The private sector's all occupations workforce was estimated at about 141 million in 2021, and its monetary size was valued at 19.6 trillion or 85 percent of the Gross Domestic Product (GDP). The depth and width of the private sector serve as a welcoming sign for entrepreneurial startup ventures to take advantage of the sector's possibilities and opportunities. The private sector functions to help accomplish the economic and technological goals of society, including the following[11]:

- To establish business entities, factories, warehouses, and other facilities.
- To create goods and services that meet society's needs and desire.
- To engage in research and development activities to improve the quality and lower the cost of current products as well as to introduce new streams of innovative output.
- To engage in the employment of workforce, deployment of capital, utilization of real estate, and acquisition and use of other productive resources.
- To improve workforce skills via training and education.
- To support the government (federal, state, and local) with

11   The role of the private sector in economic development of nations has been widely discussed in the business community and academia. For example, the Business for Goals (www. Business4goals.org) indicated that the private sector has played an important role as an engine of sustainable economic growth by employment and value creation. Moreover, in an article in the GSDRC Applied Knowledge (www.gsdrc.org), William R. Avis emphasized that the private sector an important stakeholder in both urban and economic development for being the major contributor to national income and employment.

payments of taxes and fees.

- To pay wages, salaries, fringe benefits, loan interests, and other financial spending.
- To participate in international business activities via exporting and importing of goods, services, capital, and technology.
- To support national defense, security, and space exploration with military and non-military systems, equipment, weapons, and means of transportation.

The U.S. private sector is huge as measured by financial assets, business firms, and employment. Its scope includes trade organizations, professional business associations, partnerships, sole proprietorships entities, and small, medium-sized and large companies. A simple quantitative approach which is the demand side for the country's output can be used to roughly measure the monetary size of the private sector. For example, we can state that the U.S. private sector was estimated at $20 trillion or 86 percent of the country's GDP in 2021 (Table 1).

Table 1

U.S. Gross Domestic Product, 2021

(Seasonally adjusted at annual rate, billions of dollars)

GDP Components	Expenditures/Investment	% of Total
Personal consumption expenditures	15,902.6	68.2
Gross private domestic investment	4,113.5	17.6
Government consumption expenditures and gross investment	4,160.7	17.8
Net exports of goods and services	-861.7	-3.7
Total	23,315.1	100.0

Source: U.S. Bureau of Economic Analysis, www.bea.gov. October 27, 2022.

Enterprise Performance

As stated earlier the business enterprise is an integral part of the private sector and is essential to its integrity and health. The long-term performance[12]of the enterprise is the ultimate test of its leadership's capability to manage external and internal factors that affect the success and competitive advantage of the firm. Performance (or success) factors are many and classified as macro-and micro-factors. They influence different firms differently depending on the firm's size, its resources, its strategy, and its industrial sector. External factors include the following:

- The health of the national economy (e.g., periods of depression or prosperity).
- The country's political stability.
- The rate of inflation and the interest rate.
- The level of employment.
- The structure of the market (e.g., pure competition, monopoly, oligopoly)
- The degree or intensity of market competition for the product or service.
- The consumer demand for goods and services.
- Government (federal and local) expenditures.
- The level of business investment.
- International demand for the country's products in the form of exports.
- Man-made and natural disasters (e.g., war, earthquakes).
- The rate of national technological change.

Some of the factors mentioned above (e.g., interest rate) can have strong bearing on the performance of individual businesses (such as businesses in the financial or banking sector), while other factors (e.g., technological change) can have minor, indirect influence on other businesses (such as businesses in the retail sector).

Whatever the case, business enterprise management is helpless to fully eliminate the effects of external factors on its long-term survival and success. It can, however, minimize some of the external harmful effects

---

12   A firm's performance, excellence, or success can be measured in terms of profitability, sales, assets, market share, employment size, core competency, output, or a combination of growth indicators.

with proper strategic decisions and measures. For example, the firm's management can diversify its markets, its products, its venders, and its sources of revenues.

On the other hand, internal or company situational factors that also influence the firm's market performance are largely considered controllable forces, meaning that the firm's leadership can affect them to the enterprise's benefit. The internal forces embody the firm's key critical or success factors for its survival and competitive advantage. A sample of the internal forces include the following:

- Leadership effectiveness.
- Company innovation performance.
- Company core values (e.g., business culture, ethical practices, team cohesiveness).
- Internal cooperation and communication.
- Operational competencies (e.g., innovation, market knowledge, skilled workforce).
- Critical resource sufficiency (e.g., funds, technology).
- Cost structure and price level.
- Strategic planning.
- Nature of goods and services being offered.

Purpose of the Business Enterprise

What is the justification for a business enterprise to exist? A short answer is to say it performs certain valuable functions in society; otherwise, there is no need for its existence. The most obvious functions, however, are the following:

- Offering (or producing) goods or services that meet consumer needs or desires.
- Marketing the products.
- Financing operations.
- Hiring and training a workforce.
- Managing the enterprise.

Scholars often emphasize certain functions as more important than others. For example, the father of modern management, Peter F. Drucker, believed that the business enterprise has two key purposes: marketing and innovation. In his view, marketing implies that the firm is to define and understand consumer needs. The goal should be consumer satisfaction and the firm's reward is based on its contribution to consumers.

On the other hand, innovation refers to the firm's provision of different goods and services that creates new potential for consumer satisfaction. In recent years, an increasing number of companies and entrepreneurial firms have emphasized the importance of innovation and/or disruptive innovation of their business activities.

Organizational Structure

It is widely acknowledged in the business community that employees at all organizational levels are the most important source of productivity, innovation, and growth for the business enterprise. Employees contribute within a formal structure which is also referred to as the map, skeleton, or the overall design of the organization. Organizational structure is indispensable to ensure smooth and orderly operations for the business enterprise. It helps to prevent the occurrence of conflicting directives and decisions. The structure performs additional functions including the following[13]:

- Assisting the organization to benefit from division of labor and work specialization.
- Facilitating the flow of communication and information within the organization and with the outside world.
- Identifying centers of authority and decision-making in the organization (e.g., CEO, vice presidents, directors).
- Distinguishing/labeling the different divisions, departments, or

---

13   As a system, scholars have classified the organization into four categories according to Abouzeedan and Hedner (2012): (i) a rational closed system, (ii) a natural closed system (iii) a rational open system, and (iv) a natural open system.

units.

- Identifying the organization's boundaries.

The simpler form of organizational structure is known as the functional structure whereby identical or similar work activities are grouped and placed in specialized departments or units such accounting, sales, quality control, and so on. As the firm grows in employment and product lines over time, its structure becomes more complex by moving from a simple functional form with two or three small departments to a national divisional structure (called strategic business units) based on products, services, processes, or customer types. As the firm grows even larger, its structure might take the form of a global divisional or matrix structure as is the case for multinational enterprises and large construction and engineering companies.

Two types or organizational structures are often discussed in management literature. They are the flat structure and the tall structure. The flat and tall structures are relative terms. However, the flat structure contains a limited number of managerial hierarchies (levels) as compared to the tall structure which is characterized with several levels. In general, firms with flat structures are more agile and more cost-efficient than those with tall structures because of:

- Fewer managerial positions.
- Broader distribution of authority and responsibility in the organization.
- A faster decision-making process and implementation.

The relationship between organizational structure and the organization's strategy is invariable. It is described by Professor Alfred Chandler's principle that says, "structure follows strategy." This implies that a major change in the firm's business strategy should lead to a corresponding change in its structure. Otherwise, the structure will constitute a formidable obstacle to successful implementation of the strategy. In the field of entrepreneurship, Chandler's principle suggests that would-be entrepreneurs should first develop the business strategy for their startup venture prior to the actual creation of the business.

Organizational Development

The business enterprise must always be nurtured, developed, and sustained in order to yield the finest and least cost output possible. Competitiveness of the enterprise and its excellence are the outcome of a consistent, continuous process called organizational development, that is, the process of enhancing its core and distinctive competencies and sustainable long-term growth. In other words, the purpose of organizational development is to foster long-term strategic change through human resources learning and continuous organizational improvement.

Caruso (2021) defined organization development as a process that prepares the organization to bring about a shift in beliefs, attitudes, and values to enable it to keep up with fast-paced technological and environment development. Rao and Vijayalakshmi (2000) emphasized that in today's highly turbulent private sector environment, organizational "change" has become an inevitable part of life. Business firms that do not change when the change is needed or are not sensitive to the need for change do not survive over the long run. Organizational development requires steady managerial actions in different facets of the organization including the following:

- Drive for better quality products/services.
- Greater levels of productivity and output.
- Leadership development and skills improvement.
- Innovation and technological advancement.
- Improved customer relation and retention.
- Market expansion and broader customer base.
- Lower cost and greater profit margin.
- Increased organizational capabilities and competencies.

Undoubtedly, a well-managed business enterprise is destined to grow domestically as well as internationally. As indicated earlier, business growth takes different forms including sales growth, increased market share, and superior skills. Of course, business growth must also be accompanied with profitability. The role of managerial leadership in many strategically managed firms is to accomplish these and other goals as well as seek to reach the ultimate business target of sustainable competitive advantage. On the other hand, Caruso (2021) pointed out that the techniques most widely used in the organizational development process include the following:

- Survey feedback.
- Team building.
- Sensitivity training.
- Brain storming.
- Quality circles.
- Process consultation.
- Management by objectives.

Chapter Summary

A business enterprise exists to perform important functions that include offering (or creating) innovative goods or services, financing operations, and marketing the output. Within this vein, strategies are being crafted, decisions are being made, and resources are being allocated. Organizational excellence demands the analysis of the external environment, to identify opportunities and threats, and the internal environment to identify the firm's strengths and weaknesses. The U.S. economy as measured by GDP is the largest in the world.

In 2021, for instance, the economy was estimated at $23 trillion. The huge business opportunities presented by the economy have made it possible for the establishment of millions of entrepreneurial and other businesses. Each firm has an organizational structure called the organization map or the skeleton of the organization. A business enterprise must be managed for growth and sustainable competitive advantage. The purpose of organization development is to foster long-term strategic change through human resources learning and continuous organizational improvement. The business enterprise is increasingly facing a variety of challenges that demand understanding, analysis, and planning. These challenges include:

- Rapidly emerging new technologies in various sectors of the economy.
- Society's demand for low-cost, value-added, and high-quality goods and services.
- Changing consumer lifestyle, attitudes, and value system.
- Growing danger of cyber threats and industrial espionage.
- Shortage of soft and hard skills such as managerial talent and blockchain competency.

Chapter Questions

1. What are the contributions of the private sector to the nation's competitiveness?
2. What should be the key functions of a large business enterprise such as Microsoft, Inc.? Should the functions be different in entrepreneurial companies? Explain.
3. What should be the contributions of business firms to the economy?
4. Explain the benefits of organizational development to entrepreneurial companies.
5. What are your specific recommendations for organizational development for a firm such as Starbucks, Inc. or any other business firm you are familiar with?

Chapter 6

In Search of Market Opportunities

"Opportunities multiply as they are seized."

Sun Tzu

Learning Objectives:

- Identify the nature of business opportunities.
- Know the sources of business opportunities.
- Understand the analysis of alternative opportunities.
- Study U.S industry classification.

It is common sense to point out that the business enterprise and economic opportunities are always linked to each other. This is because opportunities give rise to the creation of business firms and they, in turn, lead to the emergence of greater opportunities. Moreover, accelerated rates of economic growth pave the way for the formation of an increasing number of firms, while, on the other hand, poorly managed firms disappear as market opportunities shrink in periods of prolonged depression.

The management of entrepreneurial firms must take the necessary steps to continuously explore and cultivate market opportunities because opportunities are the source of the firm's income (revenue) and profit (earning). The business enterprise cannot survive for a long period of time without sufficient income or profit because it will be forced to consume its capital and, consequently, vanish. Searching for, and taking advantage of, opportunities is, therefore, the name of the game in the business world. Opportunity recognition and exploitation are critical tasks for the enterprise. Opportunities come about as a result of society's insatiable need and desire for goods or services.

Opportunities play a significant role in the life of societies for the following reasons:

- They give rise to the introduction of new and improved goods and services such as organic foods, smart phones, social media, and electric automobiles.
- They are the driving force for the founding of entrepreneurial companies and other businesses.
- They are the motivating factors for invention, innovation, and creative business models.
- They are the chief reason for the emergence of new technologies, industries, and economic sectors.
- They are a source of society's income and wealth accumulation.
- They contribute to the country's economic development and its global competitiveness.
- They help make living environment more comfortable and enjoyable.
- They are the chief source of job creation, spending, and national income.

What is Opportunity?

There exists a lack of a widely accepted definition of "opportunity" as is the case with many concepts within the realm of social science including economics. However, two definitions are in order:

- The Cambridge dictionary of American English defines opportunity as "an occasion or situation, which makes it possible to do something that you want or have to do or the possibility of doing something."

- Merriam-Webster dictionary defines it as: (i) "a favorable juncture of circumstances," and (ii) "a good chance for advancement or progress."

The definitions taken together imply that opportunities have the attribute of being attractive targets that can be recognized, explored, and capitalized. Moreover, it is necessary for the entrepreneur to recognize that, prior to opportunity exploitation, the following questions be addressed:

- What is the attained benefit or value to the firm as a result of exploiting an opportunity, say, for introducing or marketing a new product or service?
- What benefit or value will the product or service bring about to potential customers?
- Will exploiting the opportunity be financially rewarding for the firm?
- Are the expected financial (or other) rewards worth the efforts or the risks involved in pursuing an opportunity?
- Can the opportunity be exploited jointly in cooperation with another firm to lessen risk and gain additional support from a qualified player?

Of course, relevant information about the existence of opportunities needs to be gathered and analyzed in order to answer these and other related questions to reach a meaningful conclusion about the feasibility and profitability of identified opportunities. Market opportunities can be classified into the following categories:

- By target consumers (e.g., government agencies, businesses, individuals).
- By consumer income (e.g., low income, middle-income, high income).
- By product/service (e.g., consumer products, industrial products).
- By domestic geographic destination (e.g., local, regional, national).
- By international destination (e.g., Europe, Africa, Asia).
- By degree of risk (e.g., minimum risk, moderate risk, high

risk).

- By needed resources (e.g., minimum resources, excessive resources).

The categories of opportunities outlined above can be further classified into sub-categories for further investigation and study purposes. For example, individuals can be classified in terms of age, ethnicity, level of education, place of birth, political orientation, and so on. Geographic destination can be identified by specific state or foreign country or a group of countries with similar attributes. The issue at hand is that opportunity analysis provides the entrepreneur with a clear understanding of the nature and true value of the perceived opportunity prior to allocating scarce resources or becoming involved in costly activities.

Flow of Opportunities

Economic opportunities have the tendency to give birth to other, more diversified market opportunities. Put differently, opportunities beget opportunities. Case in point, in 2021 the world population was estimated at 7,837 million people, while the U.S. population was about 332 million, or 4 percent of the global population. On the other hand, the U.S. economy as measured by GDP was about 24 percent of the world economy. Based on data, the following observations can made:

- Because of its size and diversity, the U.S. economy provides greater opportunities to domestic and international business firms as compared to countries with smaller economies.
- "Big" economies normally tend to become bigger with the passage of time and offer greater opportunities.
- The U.S. exhibits an extraordinary level of output (GDP) relative to the rest of the world mainly because of workforce skills and the deployment of advanced technology.
- U.S. labor productivity is much higher than the labor productivity of the rest of the world.
- A higher level of productivity coupled with a large, vibrant economy can help U.S. entrepreneurial companies become more efficient and competitive relative to international entrepreneurial

companies.

As business opportunities tend to grow and expand with the country's economic growth and its technological advancement, increased spending on homeland security, for example, can lead to the creation of new business ventures and, in turn, to rising income and the opening of further opportunities. To illustrate, several years ago the television network CNBC reported that the "battle for the living room" has begun. This in turn ushers a new era for opportunities in the field of electronics. Although the major players are large corporations such as Apple, Samsung, Sony, and Microsoft, the battle for consumer demand (i) has opened windows of opportunities for newly entrepreneurial firms, and (ii) will lead to the formation of new industries and the emergence of further opportunities.

Alertness to opportunities (as is the search to unearth them) is a trait of successful entrepreneurial companies. Active search is an indispensable task, and it is the path for growth and profitability. Ideally, the search for opportunities should not be limited to a locality, a region, or even a country. Rather, it should extend beyond the national boundary whenever possible to gain access to international makers to reap their potential. The business enterprise must seek fast-growing, large markets. Wider markets offer greater return on investment in addition to being more reliable sources of future revenue. Business opportunities in the United States and around the globe are ubiquitous, diversified, and readily available to be discovered. They originate in the external environment; they are created by events, circumstances, and developments. These and other occurrences take different forms and intensity.

They are brought about by a host of factors referred to as economic, technological, social, cultural, political, and natural forces. As an example of environmental developments is that the healthcare industry decided a few years ago to embark on a huge task, that is, the digitization of health records for the entire U.S. population. The cost of the project was estimated at $300 billion. Clearly, this development has opened vast opportunities for many entrepreneurial and other firms.

Sources of market opportunities are many and include demand for goods and services from businesses, government agencies, and individuals. Opportunities, however, can be created via inventions, innovations, strategic alliances, and other forms of activities. Examples of individuals who have created immense opportunities include Henry Ford (Ford, Inc) Bill Gates (Microsoft, Inc.), Jeff Bezos (Amazon.com), Pierre Omidyar (eBay, Inc.). Steve Jobs (Apple, Inc.), and Facebook, Inc (Mark Zuckerberg and colleagues). Opportunities can be classified into the following broad categories:

Private consumption. Consumers – domestic as well as international – make opportunities happen. This is achieved through spending on a variety of goods and services including expenditures on housing, food, healthcare, and recreation. In 2021, for instance, personal consumption expenditures in the United States amounted to $15,903 million, or 68 percent, of the country's GDP. It goes without saying that the higher the level of national income (and borrowing), the larger the demand for goods and services and, consequently, the greater the opportunities for entrepreneurial firms and other businesses.

Private investment. Organizations, especially business firms, create economic opportunities by means of spending on labor, technology, materials, construction, and research and development. The various kinds of expenditures usually culminate into new and improved products and services that, in turn, lead to the emergence of further opportunities. In 2021, for instance, gross private domestic investment amounted to $4,114 million, or 18 percent, of the country's GDP. Of course, individuals also create business opportunities for others (and for themselves).

Government expenditures. The United States government (federal, state, and local) has become an important source of income for thousands of small, mid-sized, and large firms. The federal government, for example, in addition to spending on a wide array of goods and services such as defense and space projects, offers a huge amount of funds in the form of grants to individuals and small companies to encourage them to come up with new products and technologies. In 2021, for instance, federal and state governments spending on consumption and gross investment amounted to $4,162 million, or 18 percent, of the nation's GDP. As government spending increases over time, business opportunities for entrepreneurs are likely to become more plentiful.

The international economy. Clearly, overseas demand for U.S. goods and services constitutes an important source of opportunities for business firms. The list of the country's exports is large and includes such items as airplanes, steel, agricultural products, pharmaceuticals, chemicals, and financial services. In 2021, for example, total exports of goods and services amounted to about $2,540 million, or 11 percent of the country's GDP.

As is the case with exports, U.S. imports create market opportunities for thousands of domestic companies. In 2021, for instance, total imports of goods and services amounted to $3,401 million, or 15 percent of GDP. Trade deficit in the same year amounted to $861 million, or 4 percent, of the country's GDP. Incidentally, the U. S. economy has consistently experienced a trade deficit with the rest of the world for decades.

Nature. Nature in its blessing and fury plays a major role in opportunity creation. Earthquakes, tsunamis, floods, fires, and other disasters typically lead to construction and the invention of better material and technologies in the long-term. Likewise, nature's blessing in terms of weather, landscape, and other attractions can bring about lucrative opportunities for business firms.

Military conflicts. Despite the enormous human and financial toll that often result from regional or global wars, military conflicts are a source of opportunities particularly in terms of production and sales of weapons, supplies, and means of transportation. Moreover, the history of wars in Europe and elsewhere around the world reveals that military conflicts had resulted in construction booms, wealth creation, and economic progress in affected countries such as Japan, Germany, and the United Kingdom. This, of course, does not imply that national prosperity can only be achieved through armed conflicts and global hostilities.

Recognizing Opportunities

Opportunity recognition is an entrepreneurial process that requires investigation and analysis to ensure its relevance and worthiness. To this end, several questions need to be addressed such as, "does the idea, say, about the introduction of a product, project, or service represent real value to the firm and customers?" As indicated earlier, new ideas emerge from the study of the external environment and internal sources (within the firm). Whatever the source of ideas for opportunities may be, analysis, brainstorming, and management experience are required to verify the real value of the opportunity. Of course, not all business-related ideas are viable, practical, or profitable. Many ideas that initially seem to open new windows of opportunities can end up being costly, impractical, or useless. Finally, business firms recognize opportunities differently because of differences in their resources, analytical skills, market knowledge, and scope of activities.

A Methodology for Opportunity Recognition: Inside Out and Outside In

Granted that companies perceive economic opportunities differently many scholars agree that the process of opportunity recognition is complex because entrepreneurs as well as others business opportunity-seekers travel different paths in search of opportunities and how they exploit them. David W. Ewing (1968) came up with an innovative methodology for opportunity recognition. He pointed out that there are two broad approaches by which to identify potential opportunities. The methodology (or approach) is known as Inside Out and Outside In.

Inside Out refers to a firm's (or individual's) ability to "create" opportunities by choice such as inventing new products and services or modifying existing products and services. Outside In, on the other hand, refers to the ability of human beings to learn about opportunities that already exist in the external environment by whatever means possible such as by altering the shape, weight, ingredient, color, or other attributes of an existing product or service. On the other hand, market opportunities can be created by finding new applications or uses for existing products or services.

Active and Passive Search

Scholars have discussed two paths in the context of opportunity recognition: (i) active search and (ii) passive search. Active search indicates that search entities believe that opportunities reside in the environment (Outside In), and they seek to uncover them by search, analysis, and so on. For example, let's assume that an entrepreneur observed that the public in general has a strong preference for readily made fresh-fruit juice.

Let's further assume that he or she conclude that there is a lack of specialty outlets in a particular state or country that serves the beverage. The knowledge gained in this case may motivate the individual in question to investigate the validity of the perception, its business merit, and its feasibility. As is the case with active search, passive search implies that business opportunities exist out in the environment awaiting to be discovered and exploited. To illustrate, let's assume that a local U.S. dealer for used construction equipment is willing to expand his or her business but is reluctant to actively search for new opportunities.

However, during a vacation to Mexico the dealer in question learns that the country is experiencing a construction boom and, as a result, there is a growing need for second-hand construction equipment such as bulldozers, excavators, and industrial cranes. Moreover, the individual learns that the used equipment market is highly profitable and less competitive in the target country. The dealer then entertains the idea of getting involved in exporting construction equipment from the United States to Mexico upon becoming convinced of the feasibility and profitability of the project.

Fortuitous Discovery

Fortuitous discovery means that opportunities are sometimes accidently discovered. For example, while a biotechnology entrepreneurial company is in the process of seeking a cure for brain cancer, it suddenly comes across a cure for Alzheimer's or other disease. Fortuitous discoveries are relatively rare but not impossible. Examples of these discoveries include the Microwave, Plastic, Vaseline, Viagra, and the Gunpowder.

Opportunity Creation

The previous three ways of seeking opportunities – active search, passive search, and fortuitous discovery – imply that opportunities already exist in the external environment (i.e., the marketplace) and the task of the opportunity seeker is to seek them out and exploit them. Opportunity creation (Inside-Out), however, assumes that opportunities reside essentially in the minds of individuals rather than in the external environment. Examples of opportunity creation include the invention of writing, the wheel, railroads, radio, the airplane, television, and social media. Experts emphasize four methods by which entrepreneurs can identify opportunities, as listed below:

Replicate the product or service already available in the market with minor modification in its ingredients, color, size, shape, delivery, and so on.

- Innovate a product or service perceived to be desired by consumers or end users. For instance, the introduction of a product such as a new kind of aftershave cologne. Clearly, innovation calls for creativity, experience, and knowledge in the field of interest. It also requires in many instances a lengthy period of research, testing, and modification.

Acquire knowledge about a business enterprise, say a shoe factory, that is in financial difficulty and seek to purchase it.

- Invent a new product or service.

Alertness to Opportunities

Entrepreneurial business habit calls for vigilance in monitoring market opportunities. Environmental alertness is a tendency to notice information or other signals about external developments such as trends, events, or incidents that give the observer cues to be ready to analyze, evaluate, and undertake certain business projects. For instance, an entrepreneur observes that wedding planning which involves organizing groups for wedding and honeymoon occasions is gradually becoming an important and profitable industry. Alertness to the opportunity can entice the individual in question to gather more information, analyze the situation, and seek expert guidance. If she concludes that the project is profitable, then the entrepreneur may contemplate starting a wedding service venture. Peter Drucker – acknowledged as the father of modern management – and other experts have suggested the following as sources of entrepreneurial opportunities:

- Unexpected incidents that include failure or success in product or service development.
- Mismatches, which refers to the existence of a gap between what is available on the market and what is needed.
- The existence of a weak link in an existing process that needs to be corrected, fixed, altered, or redesigned.
- Environment occurrences that affect the industry, demographic, or market demand.
- New technological developments that open windows for new opportunities.

Assessing Opportunities

Opportunity assessment is a critical step prior to a decision about opportunity cultivation. It is a phase in the process of understanding the advantages and disadvantage of looming opportunities. Some firms, as they come across opportunities, tend to exploit them as fast as possible without proper assessment because they fear that the window of opportunity may suddenly close. Obviously hasty decisions in this regard can lead to undesirable consequences such as business failure or loss of capital. The following sections present some of the key issues that entrepreneurs need to consider prior to committing time and resources to exploiting potential opportunities:

Real opportunities. Common sense among other methods is essential for opportunity recognition. Let's consider an extreme case to illustrate the issue. It is unrealistic to start a venture for the purpose of selling unprocessed ocean water to customers. The opportunity in this case is imaginary because rational people are unwilling to purchase contaminated water. Opportunities exist for goods and services that meet consumer needs or desires.

Resource availability and visibility. One must have, or be able to secure, the necessary resources (e.g., capital, technology) in order to take full advantage of profitable economic opportunities. As indicated earlier, once an opportunity is identified, it should be analyzed thoroughly to determine its feasibility. The analysis should focus on at least two kinds of feasibility criteria:

- Technical feasibility, meaning that the venture (or project) under consideration can be implemented without major technological difficulties.
- Economic feasibility, meaning that the venture is expected to be profitable in the future.

Competing Opportunities

What decisions should be taken in case of simultaneous availability of competing opportunities? Let's suppose that management is presented with two attractive opportunities:

- To open a fast-food outlet.
- To join a partner (another enterprise) in founding an upscale restaurant.

Which of two alternatives should be selected? An approach known as Competitive Strength Assessment (CSA) – also called Competitive Profile Matrix (CPM) – can be deployed to help arrive at an initial answer to this issue, as discussed below:

- List five to seven key factors that influence the attractiveness of both ventures.
- Assign a rating for each factor listed. The rating varies from 1

to 10 (most important). The greater the effect of the factor on the venture attractiveness, the higher its rating.

- Assign a weight to each factor. Total weight for all factors listed is 1 (i.e., 100 percent). The weight for each factor is the same for both alternatives.
- Multiply each factor by its weight to arrive at a weighted score for each factor.
- Add the weighted scores for each alternative to arrive at total weighted scores for the alternative.
- Conclusion: highest scores for an alternative is an indication of its greater attractiveness relative to the other alternative.

Tables 1 and 2 below illustrate the procedure:

Table 1

Factors, Scores, and Weights for Alternatives A and B

Factors	Alternative A		Alternative B	
	Rating	Weight	Rating	Weight
Required Investment	5	.20	7	.20
Return on investment	6	.40	9	.40
Anticipated success	4	.20	8	.20
Degree of risk	8	.10	4	.10
Efforts needed	10	.10	5	.10
Total weights		1.0		1.0

As Table 2 shows, alternative B (joining a partner) is more attractive than option A (opening a fast-food outlet), because it has the highest total weighted scores (7.5 points versus 6.0 points).

Table 2

Weights and Total Scores for the Alternatives

Factors	Alternative A Weighted Scores	Alternative B Weighted Scores
Required investment	1.0	1.4
Return on investment	2.4	3.6
Anticipated success	.8	1.6
Degree of risk	.8	.4
Efforts required	1.0	.5
Total	6.0	7.5

Market Analysis

The business enterprise can generate many benefits from gathering, analyzing, and assessing data about competitors, customers, the industry, and the economy. Relevant data are used to develop business plans as well as other activities such as marketing, operations, and budgeting. The data also help the firm to learn about key factors that influence its competitive advantage and profit prospects. In brief, market analysis is aimed at attaining the following:

- Understanding local, regional, national, or international market opportunities and threats.
- Identifying potential customers (men, women, governmental agencies, etc.).
- knowing competitors' strategies.
- Estimating expected sales volume and revenue.
- Plotting appropriate strategy and courses of action.

Quite often, marketing strategies are designed on the basis of market segmentation, that is, dividing the entire target market into "portions" based upon certain criteria such as:

- Geographic location (e.g., city, state, country, region).
- Demographic factors (e.g., age, gender, income).
- Psychographic factors (e.g., lifestyle, personality attributes, values).

- Behavioral factors (e.g., benefits sought, brand loyalty, imitation).

The size of the market segment (e.g., number of expected buyers) is to be estimated for the purpose of developing functional strategies. The segment should be homogeneous in terms of buyers' needs. The segment should be large enough to be profitable. Marketing experts point out that once the target market is identified its necessary for management to know whether the firm's product or service is:

a) High involvement purchase, that is, whether buyers are prepared to spend time and effort searching for it, or
b) Low involvement purchase, that is, whether the product does not have much impact on buyers' life.

U.S. Industry Classification: NAICS

Economists invented an ingenious method by which to summarize a national economic system regardless of its size or complexity. The method is being taught in introductory macroeconomics courses in colleges and universities throughout the world. The method in its bare essential specifies that a country's GDP, that is, the value of goods and services produced during a given period of time is equal to its aggregate consumption (C) plus aggregate investment (I) plus government expenditures (G) plus exports (X) minus imports (M). Or simply, $GDP = C + I + G + (X - M)$.

The U.S. authorities, in addition to the GDP estimation method, use a comprehensive classification scheme by which the country's businesses, industries, and economic sectors are classified into twenty categories. Many benefits can be derived from the scheme including data collection and analysis of economic activities in the country. The scheme is called the North American Industry Classification System (NAICS).

The aggregate industry classification indicated below is sub-divided into smaller sectors of industries and these, in turn, are sub-divided into smaller classification of business activities. For example, manufacturing (NAICS 31-33) is divided into more than twenty sub-sectors that include food manufacturing (NAICS 311) and grain and oilseed milling (NAICS 3112). Moreover, food manufacturing (NAICS 311) is in turn sub-divided into animal food production (3111), dog and cat food manufacturing (NAICS 31111), and so on.

The detailed industrial classification of the U.S. economy enables entrepreneurs and others to distinctly identify the business domain of interest and, therefore, shape the venture's vision, mission, and strategic goals. An additional advantage of NAICS is that a careful analysis of components can provide valuable information to generate ideas about novel business opportunities.

Table 3

North American Industry Classification System (NAICS), 2022

Sector	Definition	Sector	Definition	Sector	Definition
11	Agriculture, forestry, fishing, and hunting	48-49	Transportation and warehousing	61	Educational Services
21	Mining, quarrying, and oil and gas extraction	51	Information	62	Health care and social assistance
22	Utilities	52	Finance and insurance	71	Are, entertainment, and recreation
23	Construction	53	Real estate and rental and leasing	72	Accommodation and food services
31-33	Manufacturing	54	Professional, scientific, and technical services	81	Other services
42	Wholesale trade	55	Management of companies and enterprises	92	Public administration
44-45	Retail trade	56	Administrative and support and waste management and remediation services	-	-

Source: https://www.census.gov/naics/.

Business Opportunities: Examples

It can be said that business opportunities in the United States and elsewhere around the world are unlimited. Entrepreneurs need to relentlessly seek or create them. In an effort to encourage entrepreneurship several websites[14] have published information about a variety of business opportunities, as indicated below:

Table 4

Examples of Suggested Entrepreneurial Business Ventures

Advertising & Promotion Services	App Developer	Personal Trainer
Refurbishing Electronics	eBooks and Guides	Care Provider
Pet Care	Voice Acting	Holiday Decorator
Errand Runner	Photographer	franchising
Business/Technology Training	Website Design	Catering Services
Commercial Arts Trading	Business Consulting	Craft Production
Wedding Service Planning	Delivery Services	Design Services
Data/Information Services	Fashion Designer	Education Services
Inspection & Testing Services	Pet Services	Publishing
Media Production & Marketing	Restaurants & Cafes	Direct Selling
Video Games Products	E-Learning	Public Relations Consultant
Drop shipping (buying products from suppliers and selling them).	Thrift Clothes	Selling on Amazon or Etsy

There are many other innovative entrepreneurial venues suitable for the establishment of business ventures, including the following:

- Designing/producing new styles of shoes (e.g., athletic shoes, boots, ladies' shoes, etc.).
- Development/production new kinds of fragrance, hair cream, or combs.
- Designing/producing new kinds of handbags, wallets, belts, or luggage.

---

14   See for example, https://commercialcapitaltraining.com/business-resources/business-ideas/40-best-business-opportunities/; https://simplicable.com/en/business-opportunity; https://www.liveabout.com/top-ten-business-opportunities-2951185; https://www.shopify.com/ph/blog/business-opportunities

- Designing/producing new styles of underwear.
- Designing/producing new styles of dress shirts, t-shirts, or children's clothes.
- Designing/producing digital paintings.
- Designing/producing jewelry.
- Designing/producing furniture.
- Designing/producing new styles of picture frames.
- Designing/producing new children's toys or games for all ages.
- Create new kinds of bread.
- Find uses for the unused (e.g., bicycles, food, cellphones, clothes).

Chapter Summary

A business opportunity makes it possible for the firm to exploit something of economic value. The marketplace is the ultimate target of the opportunity and the test of its value. Opportunities come about as a result of changes in economic, technological, and other environmental forces. Consumers, government, and businesses create opportunities. Natural and man-made disasters play a role in opportunity creation as well. Individuals can also create opportunities via invention and innovation. While military conflicts lead to human misery and suffering, they also bring about attractive opportunities.

As is the case with domestic demand, international demand for U.S. goods and services generates lucrative opportunities and stimulates the creation of new companies. Factors such as alertness, social contacts, and strategies play an indispensable role in opportunity recognition. Potential opportunities should be investigated, analyzed, and evaluated to ensure their viability and profitability. The classification of the U.S. economy into sectors and sub-sectors is a source of idea origination for new business ventures. There are a number of techniques that can be used to assess the merit (or demerit) of potential opportunities. Would-be entrepreneurs should always search for opportunities by visiting the websites of governmental agencies, corporations, trade associations, and foundations. Finally, Ardichvili et al (2003) pointed out that the major factors that influence opportunity recognition and development include the following:

- Entrepreneurial alertness.
- Information and prior knowledge of the entrepreneur.
- Social network of the entrepreneur.
- Personality traits and creativity.
- Type of opportunity itself.

Chapter Questions

1. Why do business firms search for new market opportunities?
2. How do business firms learn about opportunities?
3. Can opportunities be created? Explain.
4. What is NAICS? Is NAICS necessary? Explain.
5. What are the factors that you will need to consider a business opportunity about a human resources training contract, say, for 20 Starbucks managers?

Chapter 7

Business Strategy: Development, Evaluation, and Implementation

"The essence of strategy is choosing what not to do."

Michael Porter

Learning Objectives:

- Review the meaning of business strategy.
- Gain insight into the strategic management process.
- Discover the types of business strategies.
- Understand strategy evaluation.

Strategies are indispensable managerial tools that entrepreneurial and other business leaders deploy to assist in the achievement of organizational vision, mission, goals, and policies. Business firms without clear, effective strategies will become aimless entities in the business world. Strategy development, evaluation, and implementation is a continuous process and requires analyses, decisions, and actions. Strategies are also imperative for the orderly performance of the functional areas of business such as operations, finance, sales, quality control, and logistics. Strategies at all levels of the organization must be congruent with each other to help decision-makers attain successful strategy implementation and achieve the desired targets.

77

The Path to Strategy: Vision and Mission

A business enterprise should be administered to reach its ultimate destination of excellence echoed in achieving sustainable competitive advantage, growth, and profitability. This requires its management to create and implement the enterprise identity and its long-term strategic direction. The initial step in business strategy formulation (or identification) is the articulation of the vision for the enterprise which is a statement about its position in the marketplace and its future competitive advantage.

Examples of vision can include, "our vision is to be the best provider of healthcare in the industry." Or "our vision is to be the market leader in family entertainment."

Vision is typically expressed in a statement to inform constituencies (e.g., customers, suppliers, employees) about the firm's long-term intended target. It is also expected to influence the behavior of employees to rally them in support of the firm and its leadership. The firm's vision, mission, and goals are the building blocks for the development of viable strategies.

On the other hand, the mission statement is intended to identify the firm's business domain and its industrial base. Examples of mission statements can include, "we serve the residential mortgage business in the United States with pride and performance," or "our mission is the development of user friendly, cost-effective educational software." It should be observed that the firm's vision is about a desirable *future* state of affairs. The mission statement, however, is about the *current* state of affairs; it's about the nature of the firm's business activities and its specialization.

Desired targets

Upon finalizing the firm's vision and mission, the next step for entrepreneurs is to decide on goals and specific steps (objectives) to achieve the desired goals. Goals carry different names: (i) desired targets, (ii) desired outcomes, (iii) desired states of affairs, or (iv) desired end results. Whatever the term used is, goals in business are broad statements of management's intention to accomplish some company-related targets.

An entrepreneurial venture should not have more than four key goals. The decision to attain many goals simultaneously will cause confusion in the organization as well as pose difficulty to accomplish them because of resource scarcity, especially in newly established ventures. In any case, different goals can be emphasized at different periods of time in the life of the organization. Examples of organizational goals include, "increase sales," "elevate productivity," "improve client satisfaction," or "go global."

As the examples show, goals are broad statements of intention and are called open-ended statements. Goals must be translated into specific steps called objectives to ensure the attainment of goals. Objectives, unlike goals, are concise, short statements of intention. For instance, the following steps may be identified to achieve the goal, "increase sales":

- Hire three salespersons during the next three months.
- Augment the sales budget by an additional $25,000 during the next year.
- Train five salespersons for two weeks during the next month.
- Call-up at least 30 customers in the coming 30 days.

The Business

The first step in business or corporate strategy formulation is to identify the exact nature of the business enterprise and its business domain. A good guide in this regard is the North American Industrial Classification System (NAICS). Key questions that entrepreneurs and other business owners need to address include the following:

- What business the firm is in.
- What industry it belongs to.
- What market it serves.
- What product it offers.

- What competitive advantage it has.

Understanding these and other related issues will enable leadership to conceive the firm's mission statement and, accordingly, explore the environment, plan for the future, and boost performance. This understanding will also assist leadership devise strategic plans for business activities such as innovation, marketing, finance, and investment. Let's illustrate the nature of the firm's business as reflected in its mission statement. Suppose that an entrepreneur says that her company is in the transportation business. How accurate is this statement? The statement is accurate if, and only if, the company is involved in all of the following businesses simultaneously:

- Air transportation
- Rail transportation
- Land transportation
- Automobile rental
- Food, petroleum, water, etc. transportation
- Transportation support activities
- Other forms of transportation.

These are the main sub-sectors of the broader transportation industry. Unless the company is a truly conglomerate with extensive holdings and operations in the entire transportation industry, it will not be in all of these businesses. The essence of this example is that entrepreneurs and other business leaders must clearly define their firms' mission, that is, its business domain of operation. The mission statement, which typically consists of a few sentences, should emphasize three main issues:

- The exact nature of the firm's business (e.g., passenger air transportation).
- Is target market (e.g., United States and the rest of the world).
- Its customer focus (e.g., people).

A distinct mission statement sets the stage for the formation of business strategy for the firm and, consequently, its functional strategies. For instance, if the firm is in the airlines industry (e.g., passenger air transportation), then its mission statement may be: "We own and operate a fleet of modern airplanes. Our business is to serve all travelers, domestic and international, comfortably across the United States and around the world."

What is Business Strategy?[15]

A business strategy is a plan of action designed to plot a clear path or roadmap for the firm's future activities and prospects. A strategy can be designed for the short-term (less than a year), the intermediate term (one to three years), or the long-term (more than three years). Typically, grand strategies (business or corporate) are created for the intermediate or long-term with annual review and refinements. Vision, mission, and major goals are the main components of strategies. Quantitative and other information are generated for creating, implementing, and evaluating strategies. Many strategic decision-making techniques are used, particularly in mid-sized and large firms, including data analytics, machine learning, and econometrics.

The standard approach for strategy formulation is known as SWOT analysis. The acronym refers to internal strengths of the firm (S), internal weaknesses (W), external opportunities (O), and external threats (T). Four tables need to be created containing ten or less factors for each of the strengths, weaknesses, opportunities, and threats. SWOT analysis aims to help decision-makers arrive at alternative strategies by matching the firm's strengths with its opportunities. The analysis also helps uncover possible strategic initiatives (strategies) for the firm by viewing the contents of two components of SWOT at a time in the tables.

For example, by examining the firm's strengths (S) along with its external opportunities (O), management may identify potential courses

---

15   Several books have in recent years discussed business strategies. See for example. Arthur A. Thompson (2020). Strategy: Core Concepts and Analytical Approaches, Boston: McGraw-Hill Irwin, Inc; Fred R. David and Forest R. David (2020). *Strategic Management,* New Jersey: Prentice- Hill, Inc; Rothaermel, Frank T. (2015). *Strategic Management*, New York: Ny, McGraw-Hill Education; Hill, Charles W. and Jones, Gareth, R. (2013). *Strategic Management Theory*, Mason: Ohio, South-Western, Inc.

of action. Let's assume that the firm is financially strong (internal strengths) while consumer demand for its products is growing rapidly (external opportunity), then a strategic initiative can be to expand production facilities by constructing an additional factory. Moreover, by examining the firm's weaknesses (W) along with its external threats (T), management may consider a strategic initiative to join forces with another firm through a joint venture.

On the basis of the information revealed in the SWOT tables, management can act to minimize the firm's weaknesses and avoid (or lessen) its external threats. Clearly, the specific SWOT factors identified can be different for different industries and economic sectors. Below are examples of internal factors that at any time can represent strengths (S) or weaknesses (W) for many firms:

- Workforce skills and competencies. (e.g., accountants, engineers, managers).
- Availability of capital for investment and other purposes.
- Invention, trademarks, and patent activities.
- Coordination of activities and cooperation among business units.
- Leadership effectiveness.
- Cost structure and prices (competitive).
- Physical assets sufficiency (e.g., office space, parking, hardware, software).

On the other hand, external factors, that represent either opportunities (O) or threats (T) for the majority of business firms include the following:

- Demand for the firm's products or services.
- The country's economic environment.
- Inflation and interest rates.
- Intensity of competition.
- Laws and regulations governing the industry.
- Emergence of substitute products or services.
- Emergence of competing technologies or alternative means of production.

Types of Strategies

Business strategies have been the subject of discussion, analysis, and innovation for past decades because of their impact on the success or failure of the business enterprise. Scholars have elaborated the advantages and disadvantages to the enterprise of adopting different strategies. They also elaborated on the requirements (conditions) for effective strategy implementation as well as the criteria for strategy evaluation. Thus, many popular business strategies along with their variations have been articulated by experts in view of environmental uncertainty, intense competition, and globalization.

Strategies are classified into defensive and offensive initiatives. They include differentiation, diversification, market penetration, market development, joint ventures, outsourcing, retrenchment, and bankruptcy. Different variations exist for each strategy mainly because of:

- Changing consumer lifestyle and need.
- Different organizational vision.
- Stiff competition.
- Environmental dynamics (e.g., new technologies, products, firms).

Differentiation Strategy. The most widely deployed strategic initiative in business is the differentiation strategy in its numerous variants. Each variation is intended to single out some different (or unique) attribute of the product such as size, weight, color, performance, price, quality, convenience, speed of delivery, elegance, and so on.

The differentiation strategy can enable the firm to charge a premium price for its goods or services, as is the case with Apple phones or Rolex watches. We should note that differentiation can also add costs to the firm because of the "extra" features or enhanced quality of the product or the brand. Moreover, the strategy, if carried out to the extreme, may force some customers to refrain from purchasing the product or the service because, for instance, the features exceed their desire, need, or expectation.

Diversification Strategy. As business firms grow, they tend to expand their market domain to include additional products, customers, markets, and countries. In doing so, they tend to embrace the diversification strategy. This strategy assists the firm in expanding its offerings, sources of demand, income, and profit. The strategy ensures relative stability and growth of the firm's operations. The diversification plan can involve related products or services (e.g., producing or selling shirts and jeans) or unrelated products (e.g., automobile insurance and construction). Quite often, a diversification strategy adds burden in terms of business risk, cost, and managerial responsibilities.

Market Penetration and Development Strategies. Market penetration and market development are two interrelated growth-oriented strategies designed to expand the firm's market reach to include additional localities and customers. For example, with the help of promotional activities in such outlets as social media, newspapers, radio, and television, the firm can expand its market presence to include different counties, states, and regions. This "generic" functional (marketing) strategy is relatively low-cost, low risk, and an often-effective approach to grow the market domain of the firm.

Product Development and Invention Strategies. Successful firms seek also to utilize the so-called product development strategy as continuous innovation and perfection of its products to maintain competitive advantage. Large firms, on the other hand, also pursue invention strategies. This strategy represents an aggressive initiative that requires long-term research and development efforts and entails additional risks and capital. The long-term benefits of the strategy, however, can be enormous in terms of market share and profitability.

Outsourcing Strategy. In an attempt to reduce cost and maintain a desired level of quality, many businesses employ an outsourcing strategy by contracting certain functions such as assembly operations or customer support services to domestic or international vendors. In the

United States the majority of large companies (e.g., Dell, Ford, IBM, Walmart) depend heavily on international outsourcing. Some believe that international outsourcing can depress the demand for domestic labor and, hence, act to reduce wages or keep them artificially low. This becomes a good reason for domestic labor unions to take a stand against such a strategy.

Joint Venture, Retrenchment, and Bankruptcy Strategies. Joint venture is another growth-oriented strategy by which a firm joins forces with another to perform certain activities or undertake key projects. Joint ventures allow the partners to contribute resources such as skills, technology, and capital in the creation or development of business ventures or other projects.

Firms facing severe competition may be forced to resort to a retrenchment strategy by substantially reducing the size of the workforce or cutting spending. Finally, harsh environmental conditions may force some firms to resort to the bankruptcy strategy and abandon the marketplace entirely. However, whatever the strategy the firm pursues, it is necessary for entrepreneurs and business leaders to assess the feasibility of the desired strategy and assess its costs and benefits for the business enterprise.

The Strategic Triangle Model

As indicated earlier, strategic management is an ongoing process for the business enterprise that involves strategy formulation, strategy execution, and strategy evaluation. It also requires situational analysis for the internal and external forces that affect the firm's long-term growth and its survival. The strategic triangle model is a simplified approach to the classical model of the strategic management process. This strategy formulation approach was introduced by a Japanese scholar, Kinichi Ohmae, in his book *the Mind of the Strategist*. The recommended approach, which is also known as the three "Cs model," places the emphasis of strategy formulation on the selection of three pillars, as indicated below:

- The Company itself.
- Target Customers.
- Competitors.

As is the case with the classic strategic management model, the strategic triangle model requires analysis of the internal environment of the firm to identify strengths and weaknesses as well as its external environment with emphasis on customers and competitors. Because the strategic triangle model is a simplified approach to strategy building, it pays less attention – as compared to the classical approach – to aggregate environmental forces such as the country's gross domestic product or its political, cultural, and technological developments.

Implementing and Evaluating Strategies

Strategies are built to be implemented. Otherwise, there is no reason for their creation. Strategy execution is quite often expensive and time consuming especially for mid-sized and large firms. For example, a strategic initiative by the firm to acquire an existing business may demand substantial capital investment, cultural alignment of employees, change in organizational structure, and so on. The firm's top management, therefore, should ensure the availability of resources and other necessary conditions for effective strategy execution.

Strategy execution and strategy evaluation are two different managerial tasks although they are interrelated and intertwined. Strategies ought to be evaluated during two occasions: (i) after being formulated to ensure their viability prior to execution, and (ii) after execution to confirm their effectiveness in achieving the firm's vision, mission, and key goals. Strategies should be modified, changed, or discarded if they show lack of effectiveness. The following guidelines can assist the entrepreneur or the firm's management to ensure the viability of a business strategy:

- The strategy is formulated with sufficient knowledge of the firm's internal and external situation.
- It is legally acceptable and socially appropriate.
- It assists the firm to achieve its major goals without excessive

risk.

- It could be executed without undo financial burden for the firm.
- It enables the firm to enjoy sustainable competitive advantage.

Chapter Summary

Strategists devise business strategies to accomplish specific goals and, thus, to position the firm in the landscape of competitive advantage[16]. Strategic courses of action in the business enterprise are based on the development, execution, and evaluation of three levels of strategies, or road maps, for organizations:

- **Corporate strategy**. The strategy for the multinational corporation (MNC) such as Ford Motor Company. The MNC is typically a large company with several divisions called strategic business units. The company produces and sells different products, operates in many countries, and serves a variety of consumers.
- **Business strategy**. The strategy of a company that offers a family of related products such as the offerings of a clothing store or a strategic division of a MNC such as consumer service division in a large firm.
- **Functional strategies**. Strategies that are concerned with the company (or division) marketing, production, finance, and other main group of specialized activities.

---

16   It is held that business strategy influences the competitive advantage of the firm by way of affecting the organization's financial behavior (see for instance Wang, Can et al, 2021): The Business Strategy, Competitive Advantage and Financial Strategy: A Perspective from Corporate Maturity Mismatched Investment, Journal of Competitiveness, 13(1), 164-181}. It is also suggested that business strategy as it seeks to achieve competitive advantage is being challenged by radical discontinuity in the firm's external and internal environment that the strategy demands constant monitoring and adjustment (see for example Ghazzi, Antonio, 2013): Revisiting Business Strategy under Discontinuity, Management Decision, 51(7), 1326}. Finally, it is asserted that the firm's performance and innovation play a critical role to improve its long-term competitive advantage (see for example Ida, Farida and Setiawan, Doddy, 2022): Business Strategies and Competitive Advantage: The Role of Performance and Innovation, Journal of Open Innovation: Technology Market and Complexity, 8(3), 163.

The strategic management process is about strategy formulation, strategy execution, and strategy evaluation. Strategies should be designed to create or sustain the firm's competitive advantage and its long-term growth and profitability. Strategies should be consistent with each other and that lower-level strategies are expected to support higher level strategies.

Chapter Questions

1. What is business strategy?
2. Why do business firms need strategies?
3. What is the best business strategy in your judgement? Discuss.
4. What kind of strategies should colleges of business adopt? Explain.
5. What criteria would you recommend firms deploy to evaluate the strategies of entrepreneurial companies?

Chapter 8

Innovation and the Business Enterprise

"Innovation is taking two things that exist and putting them together in a new way."

Tom Reston

Learning Objectives:

- Grasp the meaning of innovation.
- Discuss the benefits of innovation to business firms.
- Review the process of innovation.
- Explain the types of innovation.

Innovation has in recent years become the hallmark of successful firms[17] and the weapon of their competitiveness. Innovation takes different forms and emerges in many industries. It brings fame and reward for its creators and promoters. Sources of innovation for the business enterprise are: (i) internal via experience, talent, and accumulated knowledge, and (ii) external via a process of outsourcing ideas and learning.

---

17   See for example, Wolf, Victoria et al (2021). Innovation strategies in the context of the paradigm of the five dimensions of innovation strategy, *LogForum*, 17(2), 205-211).

The practice of generating innovative ideas, products, and services with the help of outside sources has become a standard policy of many growth-oriented businesses in the United States. For example, it was reported some time ago that Netflix, Inc. awarded a $1 million prize to a group of mathematicians and statisticians for their ideas about the development of a digital tool to improve the company's movie offering.

Scope of Innovation

Innovation is a fascinating subject because it is everywhere around us. Innovation permeates economic sectors and organizations at home and abroad. Innovative business firms succeed in the marketplace, survive economic downturns, and achieve faster rates of growth. They are superior businesses to other non-innovative firms. Examples of innovative companies include Starbucks corp. (pioneered the coffee shop chain) eBay Inc. (pioneered the online auction), Amazon.com (pioneered e-commerce), Apple Inc. (the creator of the iPod and iPhone), and Google Inc. (pioneered the most efficient online search engine).

Innovative organizations are the product of the entrepreneurial mindsets, creativity, and strategic thinking of their leadership. The contribution of innovation to mankind is immense. Innovation can make the world more colorful, enjoyable, and livable. It can become a source of a nation's prosperity, progress, and competitiveness. It improves the quality of life for humans and enriches human experiences. For business firms, innovation helps capitalize on market opportunities by translating brilliant ideas into practice through the introduction of new or improved goods, services, technologies, processes, and organizational capabilities. It should be noted that innovation begets innovation[18].

18   The subject of innovation externalities (or spillovers) is discussed in the literature. It is suggested that positive externalities include the benefits that new innovations bring about to other innovators {see fro example, Bair, Stephanie P. (2022). Innovation's Hidden Externalities, *Brigham Young University Law Review*, 47(5), 1385-1433}.

Innovations (and inventions) include writing, the wheel, the radio, the internet, organizational models, and business strategies, just to mention the notable few. Innovations are not always earth-shattering events or outcomes; they may take the form of incremental (gradual), but important, improvements, say, in existing systems, methods, objects, and the like.

Conversely, innovations may well be the result of the firm's decisions to make radical (e.g., disruptive, novel, or pioneering) changes in its business processes or products. Knowledge is an essential ingredient of innovations, as is the case with experience, planning, and dedication. Innovations are complex phenomena and often considered to be mysterious. Innovations are also the result of research and discoveries.

Meaning of Innovation

Innovation, according to Oxford Learner's dictionaries, is "the introduction of new things, ideas or ways of doing somethings." The definition implies that innovation is not always an exceptional event; it could be a small change undertaken to a product, service, or process, or the like. For instance, the business model of home delivery adopted by Domino Pizza several years ago was an innovate approach (as compared to only in-restaurant service) intended to increase the company's sales, competitive advantage, and market share. A few more observations are in order about the meaning of innovation:

- The scope and range of innovation are theoretically limitless. Innovation can take place in any country, economic sector, industry, organization, product, or activity. Innovation can be manifested in physical and nonphysical aspects of objects, things, materials, and the like. For example, a uniquely designed training program on innovation is, by itself, an innovative activity.
- The outcome of innovation is something new or different from

what was considered to be typical or normal. Examples include electric automobiles, cellphones, color television sets, and synthetic rubber.

- Organizational innovation should add value to the end-user, product, process, technology, and so on. Otherwise, it becomes economically useless.
- Organizational innovation and invention typically lead to additional innovations within the organization itself as well as by other organizations. For instance, the invention of the Internet by the U.S. Army has led to a large number of innovations by many organizations, in addition to the emergence of hundreds of entrepreneurial companies with cutting-edge technologies and products.
- Innovation may or may not be an application of invention. There are many innovations that are unrelated to inventions of any kind. For example, the discovery of many medical drugs has no connection to prior inventions in the field. They are usually classified as fortuitous opportunities.

Benefits of Innovation and Invention

Innovation is a lengthy, costly, and complex process. It is a resource-based activity. For some products, such as pharmaceuticals, it can take several years for the process to come to fruition. Why do business firms exert the efforts to innovate? The benefits gained from innovation as well as invention can be substantial for the business enterprise in the long-term. Some of the major benefits are summarized below:

- Innovation enables the firm to increase output and improve quality.
- It can enable the firm to expand its market share and penetrate new geographic areas.
- It assists the firm to boost sales, revenues, and profits.
- It improves the firm's overall performance and enhances its competitive advantage.
- It can ensure the firm's long-term survival and growth.

- It can help the firm in its quest for a technological lead.
- It can pave the way for the firm for further innovations.

Disruptive Innovation versus Invention

Disruptive innovation is a strategy that deploys technology according to Clayton M. Christensen who pioneered the concept. Invention, on the other hand is according to Webster's New World Dictionary "something thought up or mentally fabricated." The definition implies that invention is something that has not been translated into a product, service, or process useful to organizations or individuals. Of course, not all inventions could be translated into products, services, or processes because they may not meet the required conditions of technical or financial feasibility.

It is believed that there are hundreds of thousands of inventions in the world that are kept on shelves or stored in computers awaiting that time to be utilized, if ever adopted. Thus, invention and innovation are two different concepts, but they are interrelated because inventions can lead to innovations. Invention and innovation reinforce each other and are necessary for the nation's global competitiveness.

Inventions are vitally important in many sectors of the economy including electronics, petrochemicals, biotechnology, communications, and automobile industries. These are the industries and sectors that enable the country to achieve its global technological leadership. In some economic sectors such as real estate, insurance, and banking, inventions appear to be less critical as compared to innovation. Industrial countries including the United States encourage business firms and individuals through grants, contracts, and other financial incentives to become engaged in invention and innovation.

Types of Innovation

The process of innovation is not uniform across all industries and economic sectors. It differs from industry to industry and from firm to firm. This is partly due to the fact that the outcomes of creative ideas vary among industries and partly because organizations follow different paths in pursuing innovations. For example, the outcomes of innovation in the pharmaceutical space are medical drugs while the outcomes in the Internet space are often software. Moreover, the methods, procedures, and resources required for innovation differ in different industries. Because of differences of outcomes and approaches employed, it is imperative for the firm's management to understand:

- Nature of the business.
- Target customers.
- Markets to serve.
- Attractiveness of opportunities created by innovation, for example, in terms of profitability and competitive advantage.
- Types of innovations needed in view of the firm's competitive environment and the associated cost for research and development (R&D).
- Best innovation practices.

Innovation is classified into categories. The Organization for Economic Cooperation and Development (OECD), for instance, classifies innovations into four groups:

- Product innovation (significant change in products' capabilities).
- Process innovation (significant changes in production or delivery methods).
- Marketing innovation (implementation of new marketing methods).
- Organizational innovation (implementation of new organizational methods).

The classification of innovations into different categories is a useful scheme particularly for the purpose of developing business strategies in different functional areas of the business such as finance and operations.

Sources of Innovation

A business firm is created to perform certain important functions such as production and marketing. The functions can be appropriate conduits or sources for the firm to gather information for the purpose of innovative activities. Firms become involved in innovative activities to take advantage of market opportunities. As alluded to earlier, market opportunities come about because of domestic and international demand for existing and new goods and services. Consumers are constantly seeking new and better goods and services to satisfy their insatiable desires. Likewise, businesses are looking for new and better tools, equipment, and software to lower costs, speed up the delivery of output, and achieve operational and managerial efficiency. Consumer, business, and government demands are the driving forces of invention in society.

Understanding the landscape of the business enterprise is essential for effective management of innovative activities. For instance, information is essential to learn about the nature and extent of demand for goods and services as well as the factors that influence the purchasing behavior of users. Sources of valuable information for managerial analysis and decision-making are briefly discussed below:

External Sources[19]

Outside sources provide important signals concerning existing or potential opportunities that encourage the firm to pursue innovative activities. They include the following:

---

19   Green innovation is becoming an important strategy for the industrial and other sectors in the United States and other developed countries. The aim of the strategy is the emphasis on the need to reduce waste as well as prevention of pollution and better environmental management {see for example, Soewarno, Noorlailie et al (2019). Green Innovation Strategy and Green Innovation: The Roles of Green Organizational Identity and Environmental Organizational legitimacy, 57(11), 3061-3078}.

- Emerging events and environmental trends provide clues about future demand for goods and services. For example, the introduction of smart telephones has created the need for a variety of software applications. Similarly, the decision of the National Aeronautics and Space Administration (NASA) to explore the outer space has spurred the demand for spacecrafts, rockets, and new kinds of innovative food and protective clothing for space travel.
- Changing consumer preferences for goods and services. For example, increasing consumer demand for healthy and organic food and for pure water has led to the establishment of new and growing ventures in the food and beverage industry.

Information/data gathering from external sources may require the firm to devise a systematic process such as the establishment of a specialized unit that monitors and analyzes external trends and developments. Firms have increasingly been utilizing such quantitate techniques as data analytics and econometrics in this regard.

Internal Sources

By instituting a proper communication and information gathering system, firms can receive brilliant ideas form their own employees. Some companies, for instance, have created a website through which employees can submit their suggestions to advance the company invention and innovation efforts. Employees have long been recognized as the most important asset for the firm because they are the main source of output, productivity, and profit. Management should encourage employees by means of incentives (financial and nonfinancial) to participate in the initiation, diffusion, and adoption of changes through inventive and innovative actions. It has long been recognized that incentives can influence the behavior of employees to become more productive, cooperative, and creative.

Innovation Deficiency[20]

What happens to a business enterprise in the absence of innovation? The simple answer is stagnation. In other words, the enterprise will experience absence of growth in employment, output, sales, market share, and profit. In all probability, the absence of innovation can lead to business failure and bankruptcy. This is because it will sooner or later be forced out of the marketplace by more innovative, aggressive, and financially healthier companies. There are other reasons for firms to be squeezed out of the market that may be related directly or indirectly to lack of innovation. These reasons include the following:

- Inexperienced leadership.
- Lack of critical resources.
- Absence of effective business strategies.
- Stiff competition.
- Prolonged economic downturn.

The Innovation Process

In the business world, innovation is a team effort whereby several individuals from different units of the organization collaborate to provide ideas about a solution for a problem that consumers or organizations face, or for a product that needs to be improved or invented. Ideas are then examined and evaluated by senior managers. An idea from among other recommended ideas is typically selected. Idea execution takes place after the necessary resources are allocation for its implementation. The outcome of the execution is assessed and, if needed, changes are implemented. Further issues about the innovation process are discussed below:

---

20   McKinsey Global Innovation Survey shows that 84 percent of executives have identified innovation as a strategic priority for their companies. However, only 6 percent of executives are satisfied with the current level of innovation in their organization {see, Innovation is king: Adopting nudge innovation to improve organizational competitive advantage (2021), *Strategic Direction*, 37(3), 9-11}.

Problem Identification

In general, innovation is an orderly, systematic process. It is launched because a problem exists that needs to be addressed. A problem is defined as a gap between the actual state of affairs and the desired state of affairs such as the gap between actual performance and desired performance. Whatever the problem may be, it should be clearly understood and defined. An example of a problem is when a business firm finds itself in a relentless decline in its market share, say, in one of its major lines of athletic shoes.

Generating Ideas

Top management may ask senior managers to study the problem and submit proposals to deal with it. Or a committee may be formed to analyze the problem. Often, employees or company consultants propose ideas to top management for consideration. The ideas can be about the introduction of new products, services, procedures, and so on. Let's assume that an investigation into the problem that was identified reveals that the product indicated earlier (athletic shoes), despite its good quality, is perceived by many consumers to be old fashioned and seemed as if it was designed for a "different generation." The problem identified in this case appears to be a design flaw of the product. Top management may suggest the following remedial options:

- Hire two new designers.
- Purchase new advanced design software.
- Purchase modern machines.
- Purchase two high-powered computers.
- Create a focus group of about twenty young people.

The figure below summarizes the general cycle of innovation and the problem-solving process:

Figure 1

The Innovation Process

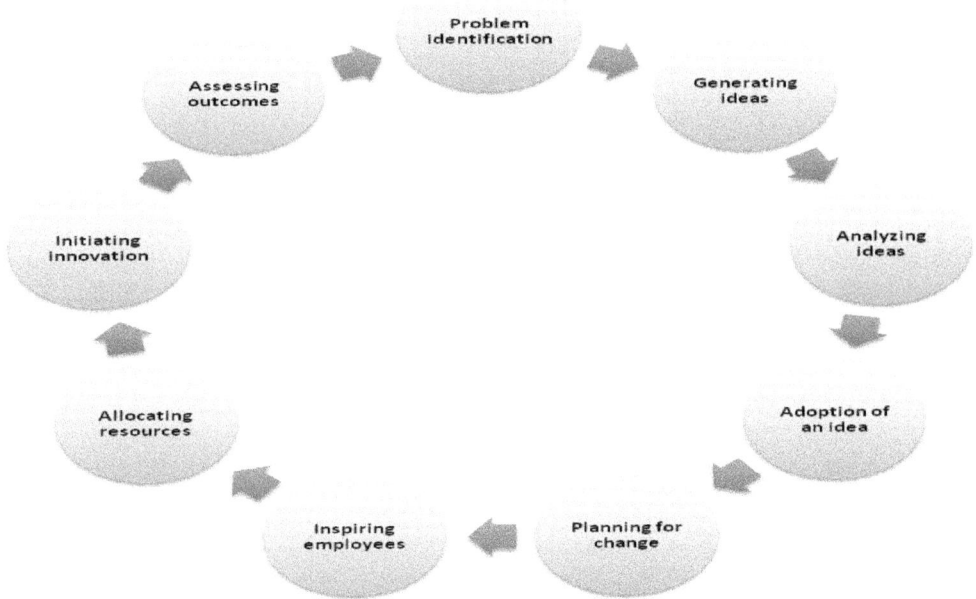

The Innovation Cycle

The American economist Joseph A. Schumpeter (1883-1950) believed that innovation is the engine of economic growth and represents the process of creative destruction, whereby new ideas replace old ones, new factories replace old ones, new technologies replace ones, new organizations replace ones, and so on. As such, innovation is a constant change in societies and around the world. It implies that organizations and entrepreneurs must understand the nature of potential change brought about by innovation, analyze it, and plan for it.

In business, the search for innovative ideas, products, services, and the like must be unabated to create new opportunities or take advantage of existing opportunities. Well-managed firms such as Microsoft, Google, IBM, and Walmart are aware of the importance of innovation as evidenced by their survival and competitive market position.

Innovation and the Company Culture[21]

At the firm's level, many internal forces motivate (or de-motivate) innovation. Company culture is perhaps the most influential of all. Company culture is usually defined as a set of values, beliefs, and business practices espoused by the firm. Company culture is instituted and nurtured by its founders. It is subsequently subject to influence and change by senior managers. Newly hired employees learn about company culture and adhere to it to avoid unnecessary conflict, confusion, and perhaps retribution.

Company culture (also called core values) vary from company to company and from industry to industry. Progressive companies espouse cultural traits that truly reflect actual business practices and their intention. Many technology-oriented firms, for instance, encourage cultural traits of innovation and strategic thinking. Below are some cultural-related aspects published by companies that appear on their annual reports or websites:

- Creativity, Innovation, and excellence.
- Environmental concern (going green).
- Customer services.
- Teamwork and communication.
- Professional and talent development of employees.
- Productivity and output growth.
- Market expansion and sales.
- Performance standards.
- Employees' initiatives, autonomy, empowerment, commitment, and responsibility.

21   Scholars have emphasized the importance of organizational culture in innovation and growth for the business enterprise (see for instance, Islam, Shk Imran and Ayupp, Kartinah (2022). Innovation is the Way Forward: The Impact of Organisational Culture on Innovation in the United Arab Emirates (UAE), *Economic Affairs*, 67(4), 463-470).

- Company growth and profitability.
- Workplace safety and security.

Building Effective Culture

Scholars have addressed the issue of effective organizational culture and the need for management and employees to adhere to a strong cultural value system. The guidance, intended for company policy development and decision-making, revolves around the following building blocks of cultural competency:

- Outline the meaning of the company's cultural attributes with examples.
- Pay attention to the organization's vision and mission.
- Create a climate supportive of cultural adaptability.
- Honor your cultural commitment.
- Train employees about the company's value system.
- Praise employees' suggestions and ideas about cultural values.
- Release employees who refuse to espouse the organization's cultural values and hire the right people.

Chapter Summary

Innovation is the engine of industrial, social, and economic progress. The domain of innovation is vast and growing. It is found in various fields including engineering, biotechnology, communication, artificial intelligence, software, and the metaverse, to name a few. Millions of inventions have been translated into practical and profitable innovations (products, services, and processes) throughout the history of mankind and, arguably, much more is yet to come.

It is the responsibility of management to initiate, direct, coordinate, and organize workforce efforts towards innovation and excellence. Indeed, the key task of management in growth-oriented enterprises is innovation; that is, offering new or improved goods or services to meet consumer demand for quality, affordability, and convenience.

Innovation knows no boundary, nationality, or culture. It is an imperative organizational process (i.e., a series of activities) intended to instigate improvement and change through the introduction of something new that is economically or technically feasible as well as beneficial. The targeted change may be minor or major depending on the desired outcome and available resources. An invention becomes innovation after being translated into a useful end result. Some scholars classify innovation into three types: technological, technical innovation, and organizational innovation.

In this book, however, all types of innovations are called organizational innovation, because they are interrelated and intertwined activities. Successful firms are invariably innovative. They can survive longer and grow faster. Information that triggers innovation comes from two sources: external (e.g., consumer need) or internal (e.g., employees). The firm's leadership plays a decisive role in the orientation of the firm to engage in innovative efforts. The benefits of innovation are many and include increased sales, profits, and growth. A firm can be forced out of the market because of lack of innovation. The process of innovation includes the following:

- Analyzing ideas
- Adoption of an idea
- Planning for change
- Inspiring employees
- Allocating resources
- Executing the idea
- Assessing outcomes.

Chapter Questions

1. How would you define the meaning of innovation? invention?
2. How do innovations come about?
3. How would you go about encouraging employees to become more innovative?
4. Which U.S. industry in your view is more innovative? Explain.
5. Do you think innovation is important for banks? Discuss.

Chapter 9

Assessing The Organizational Need for Innovation

"Creativity is thinking up new ideas, innovation is doing new things."

Theodore Levitt

Learning Objectives:

- Gain an understanding of workforce skills.
- Master a procedure for skills assessment.
- Appreciate the functions of organizational structure.
- Discover the trends in U. S. employment and job opportunities.

The vision statement guides the business enterprise to identify its business field, its industry, its target market, and its need for innovation. Grasping these domains enables the firm to conceive its long-term strategic direction and, accordingly, helps the firm explore the environment, plan for the future, and boost its financial prospect. Understanding these critical issues will also assist the firm devise viable strategies for plotting a clear path for future innovation. A key step in this direction is for the firm to assess its innovation capability and competency.

The Assessment Plan

Business firms are aware of the magnitude of their financial assets and liabilities at the end of a financial period. Some firms, however, are unaware of the shortcomings of their assets (or capabilities). Nor are they aware of the magnitude of the shortage in critical assets essential for innovation. Therefore, taking periodic inventory of available assets is an imperative task for management to identify the firm's strengths and weaknesses in light of technological development and changing consumer tastes. Detailed inventory is also an important requirement of the firm's strategic planning.

Large and mid-sized firms employ a variety of assets and other resources. Aside from the workforce such as managers, accountants, salespersons, and technicians, firms utilize a wide range of physical assets such buildings, automobiles, computers, software, and machines. Some of these assets may be outdated or deteriorated. Firms also own and leverage intangible assets including patents and goodwill. Assets inventory enables the firms to know what they have, what they need, and what the surplus is. The assessment will also assist management become aware of asset deficiencies, limitations, and strengths. A detailed inventory assessment includes the following tangible and intangible assets:

- Amount of readily available cash for deployment.
- Short-and long-term financial securities (e.g., bonds, stocks).
- Short-and long-term credit facilities.
- Other financial assets (e.g., foreign currencies).
- Managers and supervisors (numbers, skills, experience, leadership).
- Engineers and technicians (numbers, skills, experience).
- Accountants and financial analysts (numbers, skills, experience).
- Salespersons (numbers, skills, experience, leading potential).
- Other professionals (e.g., statisticians, researchers, designers).
- Machines, equipment, and tools (e.g., performance, adequacy).
- Computers and software (e.g., adequacy, performance).
- Cars and trucks (e.g., adequacy, performance).
- Need and availability of other means of production and

transportation.

- Office parking space (e.g., adequacy, convenience).
- Plants and warehouses (e.g., adequacy, safety).
- Goodwill, trademark, and patents (e.g., value, influence).
- Other intangibles (e.g., valuable external relations, core values).

A listing of assets should be followed by an assessment and evaluation of the strengths and weaknesses of each group of assets (e.g., supervisors, technicians). A firm may conclude that not all its assets are strategically relevant to innovation or related efforts. Assets can be classified into three categories (i) strategic, (ii) less strategic, and (iii) nonstrategic with emphasis on the analysis of strategic assets. The assessment assists the firm in its decision to eliminate (or minimize) weak assets and strengthen essential ones. The asset classification scheme should be based on value judgement or expert opinion.

Workforce Skills

The growing application of Artificial Intelligence (AI) technologies such machine learning as well as the increasing tendency by firms to use advanced statistical methods such as data analytics in their operations, demand a wider range of workforce skills. Workforce skills are classified into two main categories as indicated below[22]:

Hard (i.e., Technical) skills

1. Regression analysis
2. Econometrics
3. Microsoft suite (e.g., Excel, Power Point)
4. Programming software (e.g., Object-Oriented language, Scripting language)
5. Data analytics
6. Knowledge of the economy, industry, and market.

---

[22] It is emphasized that human resource management practices are significantly related to human capital which, in turn, positively affects the firm innovation {see, Mathushan, P. and Kengatharan, N. (2022). Human Resources Management Practices and Firm Innovation: Mediating Role of Human Capital}.

Soft (i.e., Interpersonal) skills

- Self-confidence
- Self-leadership
- Leadership skills
- Emotional control
- Task-orientation
- Team building ability
- Learning ability and adaptation
- Communication skills
- Human relations skills
- Conflict resolution skills
- Negotiation skills.

An Assessment Procedure

The next step in the analysis of assets is to judge the adequacy of assets essential for developing the firm's innovation plan. For the sake of simplicity, let's assume that the firm is in the business of making three classes of bicycles: custom-made, high-end, and low-end. Let's further assume that an innovative design is needed for low-end bicycles. The plan calls for a revolutionary design within a three- to six-month period. A prototype is to be tested by a focus group made up of 10 men and women in the age group of 20-30 years.

The firm's design team consists of four individuals each of whom has several years of experience. The task at hand for management is to assess the adequacy of the team to get the job done properly. A similar assessment will be carried out for two other teams if the design team measures up to the task. The teams are: (i) a production and engineering team, and (ii) a marketing and sales team to ensure the success of production and marketing of the product. Table1 below illustrates the steps of the assessment procedure.

Table 1

Judging the Adequacy of the Design Team

Team Member	Years of Experience	Performance Ranking	Required Performance Standard	Adequacy (Deficiency)
1	7	10	10	(0)
2	4	5	10	(5)
3	9	5	10	(5)
4	2	10	10	0
TOTAL		29	40	(11)

The range of actual performance raking is typically from one (lowest) to ten (highest). In this case, however, the required standard level is ten. The rankings of the performance of individuals as well as the performance standards are set forth by a team of managers. The previous table indicates that only two individuals (team members 1 and 4) can contribute to the bicycle design while the other two individuals appear to be lacking the necessary skills for the task. If the task is to be performed, then the alternatives for top management include the following:

- Only the two qualified designers should be assigned to the project.
- Hiring two additional qualified designers.
- Contracting out the design function.

Other Organizational Issues

In addition to the assessment of assets to identify weaknesses, strengths, shortages, and deficiencies, the firm needs to examine other important organizational issues. They include, for example, internal communication, information, teamwork, and leadership, as discussed below:

Communication and information flow. The aim of this kind of assessment is to identify information blockage, if any, and rectify it. In some cases, managers or organizational units do not "talk to each other." In other cases, some units or individuals think that they "own" the information and, hence, monopolize it while it is legitimately needed by others for decision-making. Undoubtedly, such practices are harmful to the business enterprise and can increase internal conflicts and retard the organization's growth.

Cooperation.[23] Innovation is usually a team effort and requires close cooperation of individuals in different teams or units in the organization. Top management must ensure smooth functioning of teams especially those entrusted with innovative activities. Moreover, sufficient resources should be allocated to these groups to perform their tasks properly.

Work environment. Clearly, the work environment must be safe, healthy, and inviting for teamwork and joint efforts. Employees are likely to be more energetic and productive in a workplace that is free of abuse, harassment, and excessive conflicts.

Leadership. Organizational leadership plays a critical role in coaching, inspiring, and leading employees. Leadership along with incentives and training are motivational factors to aspire the workforce for elevated levels of productivity and innovation.

Organizational Structure

The internal assessment should be extended to include the firm's structure, strategies, and policies. Structure is the skeleton (or map) of the enterprise. It specifies division of labor and centers of authority.

---

23   Many voices call for the necessity of achieving knowledge cooperation between governmental institutions and business firms to reinforce innovation processes in society {see for example, Zygmunt, Aleksandra (2022). The Effect of Research and Development Personnel on Innovation Activities of Firms: Evidence from Small and Medium-sized Enterprises from the Visegrad Group countries}.

It also specifies the flows of communication and information within the organization. The structure is designed to ensures the proper functioning of the organization to achieve its goals.

The most common form of organizational structures is the functional form as illustrated in the chart. In this illustration, the enterprise is divided into four departments: finance, marketing, information technology, and operations. Of course, there is no limit, in theory, to the number of departments that a functional structure can contain. In real-life, departments are subdivided into smaller units and sections.

U.S. Employment

The U.S. economy is among the fastest growing, most diversified, and technologically advanced economies in the world. As a result, the country is in constant demand for a skilled workforce in various industries and sectors. The country's employment, for instance, increased from 143 million in 2009 to about 163 million in 2019, an increase of 14 percent (Table 2). The private sector was the source for the rise in employment. While employment declined by 5 percent for state and local governments, it increased by merely 2,000 jobs for the federal government during the period under consideration.

The data imply that college graduates and other individuals planning to seek employment in the future should prepare themselves to acquire knowledge and skills demanded for occupations or careers either as employees in the private sector or as entrepreneurs. This is because of the anticipated scarcity of employment opportunities in governmental agencies. Employment data also imply that the national economy was vibrant and conducive for private investment that helped create millions of new job opportunities.

Table 2

U.S. Employment by Major Economic Sectors, 2009-2019

(Thousands of Jobs)

Sector	2009	% of Total	2019	% of Total	% Change 2009-2019
Total	143, 036	100	162,796	100	14
State and local government	19,723	14	18,759	12	(5)
Federal government	2,832	2	2,834	2	(0)
Agriculture, forestry, fishing, and hunting	2,012	1	2,304	1	15
Manufacturing	11,848	8	12,840	8	8
Construction	6,017	4	7,492	5	25
Mining	643	1	685	0	7
All other sectors	99,961	70	117,882	72	18

Source: Table calculations are based on data provided by the Bureau of Labor Statistics, https://www.bls.gov/emp/tables/employment-by-major-industry-sector.htm.

A review of Table 2 shows that the share of state and local governments in total employment in 2019 was relatively high (12 percent), although it declined from 14 percent in 2009. It appears that this sector of the economy is in need for greater development of workforce skills in addition to increased utilization of modern technology to further enhance the sector's performance effectiveness and its productivity. The share of mining in total employment was minor in 2019 (less than one percent), as was the share of agriculture, forestry, fishing, and hunting. The negligible share of mining in total employment is largely attributed to:

- Closing of many mining operations in the county because of environmental concerns and the increased utilization of other sources of energy.
- Resource depletion of the mines.
- Declining output prices.

The low employment share of agriculture, forestry, fishing, and hunting in total employment is due to greater deployment of mechanization and other technologies. It is interesting to observe that the construction sector experienced a large jump in employment (25 percent) from 2009 to 2019, an indication of the country's improved economic activities and increased demand especially for housing. Excluding utilities and self-employed, ten economic sectors (out of twenty) contributed more than 70 percent to the country's employment in both 2009 and 2019 (Table 3).

In 2019, the professional and business services sector was the largest single source of employment in the United States (21.3 million), followed by healthcare and social assistance (20.4 million), leisure and hospitality (16.6 million), and retail trade (15.6 million).
The growing demand for employees coupled with the emergence of new technology will necessitate further development of workforce skills and upgrade of its capability in both hard and soft skills. Educational institutions, business organizations, and governmental agencies can play a critical role in this regard. On the basis of recent employment statistics, it seems the following are among the skills expected to be in high demand in the near future:

- Management/leadership/general business
- Innovation/critical thinking
- Accounting/finance software application and analysis
- Computer programing/data analytics/artificial intelligence
- Advanced quantitative analysis (e.g., econometrics)

Table 3

Selected Employment Sectors, 2009-2019 (Thousands of Jobs)

Employment Source	2009	2019	% Increase (Decrease)
Professional and business services	16,634	21,313	28
Healthcare and social assistance	16,540	20,413	23
Retail Trade	14,528	15,644	8
Leisure and hospitality	13,078	16,576	27
Self-employed (nonagricultural)	8,995	8,782	(2)
Financial activities	7,838	8,746	12
Other services (unclassified)	6,150	6,714	9
Wholesale trade	5,521	5,903	7
Transportation and warehousing	4,225	5,618	33
Education services	3,091	3,765	22
Information	2,804	2,859	2
Utilities	560	549	(2)
Total	99,964	116,882	17

Source: Table calculations are based on data provided by the Bureau of Labor Statistics, https://www.bls.gov/emp/tables/employment-by-major-industry-sector.htm.

The national goal of maintaining a global competitive advantage makes it imperative for the U.S. workforce to be skillful, productive, and innovative. While some skills are deemed essential for all occupations and sectors of the economy (e.g., effective communication), other competencies (e.g., stock analysis) are industry or company specific.

The distinction between hard and soft skills is blurred because of the absence of precise distinguishing factors between them. In general, hard skills refer to the individuals' capabilities in performing specific technical tasks related to organizational functions such as marketing, finance, and quality control. On the other hand, soft skill (also called people skills) are competencies often related to personality attributes of the individuals such as leadership, innovation, cultural intelligence, and communication.

For many years, workforce skills (and under-skills) have been the subject of discussion by many circles. Different aspects of skills have been debated with the aim of bridging the skills gap. For example, a study conducted by Laboissiere and Mourshed (2017) of McKinsey and Company showed that about 40 percent of American employers say they cannot find people with the necessary skills they need even for entry-level jobs.

Chapter Summary

Business firms must assess the internal and external environment to draft their strategic direction. A goal of the internal situational assessment is to identify the firm's readiness to undertake inventive and innovative activities and rectify the situation, if needed. The assessment focuses on the firm's assets, leadership, systems, procedures, and policies. External forces such as government spending, competition, and consumer demand can influence the internal situation of the firm. A number of techniques are available to be used in the analysis including Competitive Strength Assessment (CSA). The skills gap is a serious problem that the U.S. economy must confront and settle to maintain its long-term growth and competitiveness. Likewise, many companies experience shortage in highly qualified personnel in various positions. Solutions revolve around innovative courses of actions to rapidly enhance workforce competencies in critical soft and hard skills with the help of education, training, apprenticeship, internship, and the like. Innovation in many industries faces hurdles that need to be addressed in cooperative efforts between business leaders and government agencies.

Chapter Questions

1. Explain the need for the internal skills assessment of the firm.
2. What are the most important skills for the hospitality industry?
3. As a consultant, how would you go about assessing small firms' readiness for innovation?
4. What are the most demanded skills in the financial sector?
5. What are the causes of skills shortage in the country?

Chapter 10

The Road to Disruption

"Those who disrupt their industries change consumer behavior,
alter economics, and transform lives."

Heather Simmons

Learning Objectives:

- Understand the disruptive innovation strategy.
- Review disruptors' businesses.
- Identify disruptors' sources of funding.
- Discuss the influence of disruptive innovation on the economy.

Economic, technological, social, and other environmental changes in the United States and elsewhere around the world are likely to bring about huge market opportunities for disruptive firms because of increased consumer demand for cheaper and more innovative products. Disruptive innovation is a relatively recent field of innovation, study, and practice.

This chapter is designed to dive into the field to discuss the business domain, vision, and technology of the emerging companies that have attracted the attention of investors in recent years and commanded a substantial amount of financing. The 2021 CNBC 50 disruptor companies, represents the source data for the discussion. The discussion can help newly established entrepreneurial and other firms develop disruptive innovation strategies to help them grow and attain a competitive advantage.

The theory of disruptive innovation, which was pioneered by Clayton M. Christensen and his colleagues in the 1990s, has attracted the attention of executives and scholars[24] because of its far-reaching implications for business creation and destruction[25]. Accordingly, disruptive innovation is about a strategy that deploys a technology, not about the technology per se. In essence, disruptive innovation involves the following business strategies:

- Introduction of innovative, low-cost, products.
- Creation of new markets.
- Deployment of new business models.

The Disruptors

Innovative entrepreneurial companies in the United States have in recent years become the dominant feature of economy. Many of these firms are young, visionary, and well-funded as evidenced by the CNBC list of disruptor companies (see the Appendix). A range of factors have contributed to the emergence of creative ventures, including the following:

- The entrepreneurial mindset of the U.S. society and its innovative spirit.

24   For example, it is said that disruptive innovation affects businesses and sectors in varied and complex ways because it has substantial positive impact on real-world practices {See, Martinez-Vergara, Sucet J. and Valls-Pasola, Jaume (2021). Clarifying the disruptive innovation puzzle: a critical review, *European Journal of Innovation Management*, 24(3), 893-918}.
25   Weinreich, Simon et al (2022) pointed out that disruptive innovation has the potential to fundamentally change the competitive landscape of markets in many courtiers. Specifically, established companies are confronted with the threat of being forced out of the market by more innovative rivals. Nevertheless, companies also can control markets development by aggressively pursuing disruptive innovation themselves.

- A vibrant and growing economy.
- The growing prosperity of U.S. consumers.
- Willingness of consumers to purchase new, high quality or improved goods and services at relatively affordable prices.
- The country's legal, political, and investment environment that have made it conducive for entrepreneurs to launch a variety of successful business ventures.
- Availability of a talented workforce.
- Accessibility to sources of finance for sustainable, innovative ventures. Sources of funds include venture capitalists, angel investors, and financial institutions.

In 2021, CNBC published its annual list of 50 disruptor companies. Briefly, the list was created on the following basis:

- Companies that received funding after January 1, 2006 were invited to be nominated for possible inclusion in the list.
- The companies' data and other essential information were analyzed by a group of 47 experts called the advisory council.
- A group of experts analyzed the data and other information submitted by the companies.
- The selected companies were ranked.
- The selection process was conducted based on several criteria that included the company's total workforce, diversity measures, and nature of technology deployed.

Table 1 below shows the economic sector classification of the disruptive companies. The table demonstrates that disruptive innovation can occur in any segment of the economy:

Table 1

Sector Distribution of the 50 Disruptor Companies, 2021

Industry	Number of Companies	Percentage of Total
Fintech	11	22
Healthcare	7	14
Logistics	5	10
Media	3	6
Cybersecurity	3	6
Enterprise Technology	3	6
Food	3	6
Education	2	4
Transportation	2	4
Biotech	1	2
Agriculture	1	2
Travel &Leisure	1	2
Aerospace/transportation	1	2
Retail	1	2
Recycling	1	2
Automotive	1	2
Insurance	1	2
Telecom	1	2
Materials	1	2
Construction	1	2
Total	50	100

Source: the table is constructed from the original CNBC data.

Sector Distribution of the Disruptors

The disruptors have created a distinct market position in twenty growing sectors. These and other disruptors will undoubtedly pave the way for the emergence of more disruptors in the future. In any event, the sectors indicated above represent a sample of potentially lucrative business opportunities in the country.

As Table 1 illustrates, the majority (22 percent) of the companies are in the fintech industry, followed by healthcare (14 percent), and logistics (10 percent). Business firms in media, cybersecurity, enterprise technology, and food occupied the fourth position on the list of disruptors. The inclusion of the companies in the list of disruptors is an indication of the following:

- Uniqueness of the companies' products and technologies.
- Expected growth of market demand for the companies' products.
- Willingness of venture capitalists and other investors to fund the companies.
- Optimism about the future health and stability of the national economy.

The Disruptors' Businesses

Learning about the business domain of disruptive companies can help would-be entrepreneurs to identify the scope of potential new opportunities. However, the analysis of the disruptors' business reveals that many of them have carved a distinct market niche in certain economic sectors/industries. Below are examples of the 50 disruptors' businesses:

- Financial transactions platforms (e.g., stocks, digital currencies) that link client's bank account to the company's trading system.
- Domestic and international money transfer among individuals or between individuals and companies or among companies.
- Micro lending ($50-$500) to low-income individuals or lending to would-be entrepreneurs unable to secure bank credit.
- Processing, monitoring, and fraud prevention payments.
- AI-based process for blood testing.
- Software to detect organizations vulnerability to malware.
- Meat alternatives for human consumption.
- Eggs that contain no cholesterol and less saturated fat.

- Online nanodegree programs (e.g., a semester long) in advanced technology such as AI, machine learning, the internet of things, and so on.
- Batteries that last longer and cheaper.
- The use of bio-based recyclable fiber.

The Disruptors' Technologies

The majority of disruptor companies reported to CNBC that they deploy at least two of the following technologies:

- Cloud computing.
- Machine learning.
- Deep learning.
- The internet of things.
- Robotics.
- Artificial intelligence.
- Autonomous vehicles.
- Facial recognition.
- Nanotechnology.
- Blockchain.

The Disruptors' Vision

Vision is a key component of business strategy and conveys the ultimate purpose of the business enterprise. Typically, entrepreneurs and business leaders express their vision in a concise, clear statement. Below are examples of vision developed by disruptors:

- Enable the masses to participate in the nation's financial sector including digital currencies, stocks, and other financial instruments.
- Facilitate customers' payments to venders in a safe and user-friendly manner.
- Create worldwide payment systems characterized with reliability, accuracy, and speed.
- Provide individuals with at-home medical device kit for health

examination/disease testing.

- Make goods and services available everywhere, anytime on-demand.
- Decrease greenhouse gas emission with the help of cloud computing, deep learning, and other AI-enabled technologies.
- Build a road to Mars as an industrial center.
- Transport food and other produce economically and without waste.
- Help creators (e.g., painters, musicians) sell their output on the company's platform directly to interested parties without the use of intermediaries.
- Change the eating habit of humans by eliminating the need for food from animals.
- Offer short-term educational programs sought by the business community to enhance employees' skills competencies in such areas as deep learning, the internet of things, tableau, and enterprise security.
- Production of goods and services that do no harm to the environment.

The Disruptors' Funding

As evidenced by the amount of funding made available to the 2021 CNBC 50 disruptors,

venture capitalists and other investors appear to be generous in rewarding innovative, disruptor companies with hefty financing. For example, the range of disruptor funding was from $19 million (healthcare) to $24.9 billion (transportation). The amount of financing awarded should provide plenty of encouragement to would-be entrepreneurs to think strategically for identifying innovative ventures that add value to target markets and end-users. Funding criteria included the following:

- Uniqueness of the venture's technology and its business model.
- Innovative capability of the venture.
- Demand anticipation for the venture's products.
- Credibility, skills, and experience of the venture's entrepreneur(s)

and the team.

- Competitive advantage of the venture and its ability to achieve sustainable growth.
- Management vision and the strategic posture of the venture

Lessons Learned from the Disruptors

The information discussed in this chapter reveals interesting lessons for students of business and would-be entrepreneurs, as discussed below:

- Lucrative market opportunities are often found for products that satisfy unmet consumer needs. Consumers have needs for goods and services especially for products that exhibit such attributes as convenience, price suitability, speed of delivery, user-friendliness, rarity, or so on of value-added features.
- AI-related technologies have increasingly become the prerequisite trait of successful entrepreneurial businesses. Technologies include machine learning, deep learning, cloud computing, the internet of things, and the like. The kind of technology to be deployed in business firms depends largely on the nature of products contemplated, the intensity of competition, required financing, and target markets/customers.
- Familiarity with the working of the business enterprise such as prudent management, creative thinking, opportunity identification, and awareness of appropriate technologies.
- Willingness to assume calculated business risks.

Chapter Summary

The strength and resilience of the U.S. economy - coupled with the business spirt of millions of individuals and the willingness of investors to finance unproven ventures - have all made it possible for creative individuals to launch ventures and sustain their growth. These companies are generally powered by modern, advanced technologies that include deep learning, robotics, and the internet of things.

They operate in rapidly growing economic sectors of the country such as healthcare and cybersecurity and have curved unique market niche in each sector such as remote health diagnostics (telehealth) and trading in digital currencies (e.g., bitcoin). Many of the companies have enjoyed substantial financial resources that enabled them to achieve sustainable growth. The founders are visionary in that they identified lucrative market opportunity and have attracted competent managerial teams as demonstrated by the companies' increased market valuation after founding.

Chapter Questions

1. What is disruptive innovation?
2. Discuss the differences between invention, innovation, and disruptive innovation.
3. Which is more important to U.S. economy: invention or disruptive innovation? Explain.
4. How should entrepreneurial firms pursue disruptive innovation?
5. Will you consider starting a disruptive company? Why? Discuss.

Appendix

2021 CNBC Disruptor 50 Companies

Robinhood	Gojek	Bestow
Stripe	CLEAR	Gopuff
Discord	TALA	Databricks
SentinelOne	Flutterwave	Ripple
Didi Chuxing	Thrasio	Plaid
Brex	Relativity Space	Nubank
Marqeta	Impossible Foods	Flexport
Chime	AMP Robotics	Flock Freight
TytoCare	Neteera	Eat Just
ElevateBio	Cockroach Lab	Movandi
K Health	Cityblock Health	Footpring
Convoy	Udacity	Airtable
Checkout.com	Apeel	BlocPower
Indigo Ag	Sight Diagnostics	Patreon
Snyk	Cybereason	Guild Education
Tempus	Clubhouse	Heal
Lineage Logistics	Sila Nanotechnologies	-

Source: 2021 CNBC Disruptor 50 companies, www.cnbc.

Chapter 11

Management Schools of Thought[26]

> "Theory is needed to tell you where to look."
>
> Marcus du Sautoy

Learning Objectives:

- Learn about the major schools of management thought.
- Appreciate the importance of theorizing in management.
- Explain the benefits of a systems approach to business firms.
- Understand the quantitative approach to management.

Over the past 100 years, the field of business management has witnessed significant developments such as the emergence of the multinational corporation, intensity of market competition, technological advancement, and increasing environmental turbulence. As a result, management has emerged a recognized discipline of social sciences like economics, psychology, and sociology with colleges and universities around the world offering graduate and undergraduate degrees in this and related body of knowledge.

---

26   Management, as theory and practice, is continuously changing as well as stimulates organizational attitude changes {Druqus, Liviu (2010). On Management: Is it Scientific Management? No! Is it Management Science? No! Is it Changing Management? YES! *Economy Transdisciplinarity Cognition*, 13(1), 5A-6A}.

Management as a discipline encompasses theories, principles, techniques, and applications. A variety of management and organizational issues are annually discussed in professional conferences, seminars, business forums, and workshops. Several management journals have also been published[27]. The discipline is primarily intended to guide managerial decisions, actions, and practices of executives, managers, supervisors, entrepreneurs, and business owners.

Different schools of thought in the United States and other industrial countries have contributed to the development and dissemination of the discipline. Our goal in this book is to briefly review some of the major schools of thought to learn about their contribution and influence on the management of modern organizations. This review can help the reader understand different approaches and strategies to managing human, intellectual, and physical resources in organizations and, hence, become a better leader and strategist in a dynamic, highly competitive global environment.

Scholars (and practitioners), because of varying backgrounds and experiences, have viewed the practice of management from different perspectives and suggested a host of ideas to decision-making and the management of the business enterprise. In the final analysis, it can be said that there isn't one "best" approach to decision-making, resource allocation, or attaining organizational excellence. However, organizational leaders and other decision makers should select courses of action that yield the best outcome for the organization with minimum expected risk. This can be achieved with the help of wise judgment, experience, and the deployment of market analysis in conjunction with quantitative techniques such as data analytics and econometrics.

Scientific Management

The oldest and most prominent school of management thought is known as the scientific management school. The school has had significant influence on the practice of management in many companies in the

---

27   For example, Academy of Management Journal, Academy of Management Review, Journal of Management, Journal of Business Research, European Journal of International Management, European Journal of Management, and Journal of Management Research and Analysis.

United States and other industrial nations. It acquired its name because it emphasized the deployment of "scientific" methods in managing organizational resources and operations, especially production and assembly activities.

The school emphasized the importance of organizational performance in terms of work efficiency, productivity, and output. Specifically, the school teaches that top management should embrace "scientific" methods in the workplace mainly at the factory level to improve labor productivity, lower cost, and increase production level. The school promoted, among other things, the following set of recommendations and actions:

- Proper selection, supervision, and training of the workforce.
- Use of clear standards and procedures in the workplace.
- Utilization of time and motion studies for improving labor productivity and increasing the level of output.
- Implementation of a reward/punishment system to improve organizational performance.

Several prominent individuals had been instrumental in the emergence and popularity of the scientific school. Frederick W. Taylor (1856-1915)[28], Frank Gilbreth (1868-1924), and Lillian Gilbreth (1878-1972) were among the original contributors to this school.

Administrative Management

The Administrative Management school is believed to have been pioneered by Henri Fayol (1842-1925)[29]. His writings were mainly

28   It is argued, contrary to popular believe, that Fredrick Taylor's writings about labor-management relations in 1900s had portrayed managers as naturally good people who were not self-interested in pursing their functions {see for example, Wagner-Tsukamoto, Sigmund (2008). Scientific Management revisited: Did Taylorism fail because of a too positive image of human nature? *Journal of Management History*, 14(4), 348-372}.
29   The contribution of Henri Fayol to management analysis, management education, and understanding of managerial functions is widely acknowledged

focused on the management of the business enterprise as a whole system rather than on boosting workers' output and productivity as is the case with scientific management. Fayol was the first author to discuss key managerial functions that include the following[30]: Planning, organizing, leading, coordinating, controlling, staffing, and evaluating. These functions constitute the key responsibility of managing modern organizations especially for executives and managers at the middle and top management levels. Henri Fayol and other scholars of the classical school of management such as Chester Barnard (1886-1961) played a pivotal role in the advancement of management discipline and its prominence in social sciences. He emphasized that:

- Executives should define the purpose of the organization and establish formal communication system to disseminate information.
- A distinction should be made between formal organization (i.e., organizational structure) and the informal organization (i.e., relationships among employees).
- Organizational success requires coordination of activities among all levels of management.

The Human Side of the Enterprise (Human Relations)

Many contributions and approaches have emerged over the years that are concerned primarily with the human side of the enterprise and its internal dynamics such as conflicts, interactions, and relationships. Among the main contributors to this school of thought is Douglas McGregor (1906-1964). McGregor had a strong belief in the intention and ability of employees to positively contribute to

---

{see for example, Wren, Daniel A. (2003). The Influence of Henri Fayol on Management Theory and education in North America: 1. Early Recognition and the Coubrough Translation, 2. The Storrs' Translation and Management Education in North America, 3. Renewed Interest and Empirical Tests of Fayol's theory Conclusion, *Enterprises of Histoire*, 34, 98-107}.

the success of their organizations. He introduced the widely known Theory X and Theory Y. Both theories according to McGregor are about assumptions that many managers make about subordinates[31].

According to theory X, the average employee tends to be lazy, dislikes work, and avoids available opportunities to assume organizational responsibilities. To induce the individual to behave in a positive and productive manner, he/she must be subjected to punishment or threat of punishment. Theory Y, on the other hand, is about the good intention and dedication of employees to serve their organizations to the best of their ability. The typical employee, according to his theory, is willing to work hard, exert the necessary efforts, and seriously view work responsibility. Organizations, however, need to maintain a conducive workplace environment in order to bring about the optimal efforts of their employees.

On the other hand, Abraham Maslow (1908-1970) introduced the so-called hierarchy of needs theory. He postulated that individuals in general have five hierarchical progressive needs that demand complete satisfaction. They are ranked from the lowest to the highest needs. In organizational settings, it is postulated that, once a need is fully satisfied, it would no longer act as a motivator for the individual

---

31   It is reasoned that Douglas McGregor's landmark book, The Human Side of Enterprise in which he introduced Theory X and Theory Y, has changed the path of management thinking and practice by questioning key assumptions about human behavior in organizations {see, Kopelman, Richard E. et al (2008). Douglas McGregor's Theory X and Y: Toward a Construct-valid Measure, *Journal of Management Issues*, 20(2), 159-160}. On the other hand, it is mentioned that McGregor's general "Theory X Theory Y" are well known, but seldom are they compared to management practices in modern organizations {see, Head, Thomas, C. (2011). Douglas McGregor's legacy: lessons learned, lessons lost, Journal of Management History, 17(2), 202-216}.

concerned but a higher need will act as a motivator. The needs from the lowest level to the highest level are indicated below[32]:

1. Psychological needs (e.g., food, water, shelter).
2. Safety needs (freedom from physical and emotional harm).
3. Social needs (e.g., the need to love and be loved).
4. Esteem needs (e.g., the need for recognition).
5. Self-actualization needs (to be what one's wants to be).

The Systems Approach

The term "system" is a powerful concept in sciences and real-life because everything including the universe, the sun, the moon, and organizations can be dissected and studied from this holistic approach. A system, according to Merriam-Webster dictionary, is "a regularly interacting or interdependent group of items forming a unified whole." Systems have been classified into different categories including open versus closed, social versus natural, small versus large, developed versus underdeveloped, and so on. Like other entities, business firms can be viewed from the perspective of systems theory.

This means that the entire firm is a subsystem of its industry, the industry is, in turn, a sub-system of the economic sectors it belongs to, and the sector itself is an integral part of a larger system which is the domestic economy. Viewed as a system, the firm consists of sub-systems such as units, departments, divisions, teams, and individuals. The internal components of the firm are simultaneously systems and

---

32   Research findings indicate that social media adoption follows Maslow's hierarchy of needs theory. Moreover, the theory fits well with the proposed social media adoption model {see, Ghatak, Sanchita and Sing, Surabhi (2019). Examining Maslow's Hierarchy Need Theory in the Social Media Adoption, *FIIB Business Review*, 8(4), 292-302}. Besides, a study found that bank employees follow Maslow's motivational theory and that the theory holds across national cultures {see, Rahman, Md H. and Murullah, Sheikh M. (2014). Motivational Need Hierarchy of Employees in Public and Private Commercial Banks *Central European Business Review*, 3(2), 44-53}.

sub-systems. A subsystem of the firm, say, an employee by himself/herself can be considered a system comprised of many sub-systems such as hands, legs, the eyes, and so forth.

The relevance of systems theory to managing organizations is that leadership should view the organization, as consisting of many interrelated and interdependent components, as an open system that influences and is being influenced by other systems. An implication is that in making strategic decisions, for example, relevant internal and external systems (e.g., macro factors) and subsystems (e.g., micro factors) need to be taken into consideration. Systems theory[33] has been an important factor, for instance, in the development of Strengths, Weaknesses, Opportunities, and Threats (SWOT) analysis, a technique commonly used to develop business strategies. The essence of SWOT analysis is the conviction that the firm's performance is a function of its subsystem (the internal situation) and external subsystems (environmental influences).

The Quantitative Approach

As business firms became larger and more complex in their operations, new approaches and more sophisticated techniques were needed to guide managerial decisions and resource allocation. Some scholars called for analyzing managerial problems in the context of systems framework. Others called for the utilization of advanced quantitative techniques such as regression analysis, econometrics, and data analytics.

More recently, the emphasis has also been on the deployment of Artificial Intelligence (AI) technologies such as machine learning and sophisticated software especially in making

---

33   Systems theory has been deployed in analysis in many fields of natural and social sciences including the study of entrepreneurial ecosystem {see for example, Daniel, Lisa J et al (2022). Understanding entrepreneurial ecosystems using complex adaptive systems theory: getting the big picture for economic development, practice, and policy, Entrepreneurship and Regional Development, 34(9/10), 911-034}.

corporate strategic decisions. Undoubtedly, quantitative techniques can help management make more effective decisions concerning organizational functions in production, finance, marketing, and other areas in addition to assisting managers in carrying out their responsibilities in planning, controlling, coordinating and other key managerial tasks.

Some of specific methods that have become popular in various industries include linear programing, business simulation, and statistical sampling. Much of the business quantitative techniques were developed during the 1940s and 1950s to assist U.S. military efforts as well as to assist the multinational enterprise in decision-making.

Other Major Contributions

The list of outstanding contributions to the development of management thought is long and rapidly growing; it includes the following:

- Bureaucratic Organizations (Max Weber).
- Total Quality Management (W. Edwards Deming).
- Management by Results (Peter F. Drucker).
- The Five Forces Model and Generic Competitive Strategies (Michael Porter).
- The 7-S Framework (Tom Peters and Robert Waterman, Jr.).
- Balanced Scorecard (Robert S. Kaplan and David P. Norton).

Chapter Summary

Management has been viewed from two distinct perspectives: (i) as a group of people (top management, middle-management, and first-line management), and (ii) as a body of knowledge, that is, as a field of research, teaching, and learning which consists of theories, principles, and techniques. As a body of knowledge, management has grown rapidly during past decades as a result of scholarly contributions with the publications of various books and academic articles as well as the contributions of visionary business leaders.

The contributions have included the development of theories to advance managerial understanding of management best practices, decision-making, and efficient resource allocation. Among the major management theories have come to be known as scientific management, administrative management, human relations, systems management, and quantitative methods.

Chapter Questions

1. What is theory?
2. What are the criteria for "best" theory?
3. Are theories necessary in managing organizations? Explain.
4. What are some management theories?
5. What is the difference between theory and strategy?

Chapter 12

The Theory of Inventive Problem Solving (TRIZ) and its Role in Managerial Strategic Decisions

"To invent, you need a good imagination and a pile of junk."

Thomas A. Edison

Learning Objectives:

- Discover TRIZ.
- Know the different types of problems.
- Grasp the concept of an ideal final result.
- Understand the application of the 40 principles in management.

The business firm is born in order to survive and grow. Growth is a natural outcome for a well-managed firm. A stagnant firm is doomed. As already alluded to elsewhere in the book, business growth takes many forms, including increased sales, revenue, profit, employment, assets, and market share. Growth can be strategized and controlled. It can be haphazardly executed and excessively costly.

Business growth necessitates the adoption of an orderly process for strategy identification, formulation, execution, and evaluation. Strategies, as creative plans of action, must be compatible with the firm's internal resources as well as with its external environment. What makes the efforts for attaining organizational growth challenging is that growth can be accomplished internally by means of organic expansion or external through acquisitions, mergers, joint ventures, and other modes of business expansion.

Moreover, growth-oriented strategies are many and diverse. The decision to select a strategy from among an array of potential alternatives should be based on a reliable, systematic, and scientific methodology. After all, the chosen strategy is a decision in innovative problem solving.

This chapter explains the nature of the Theory of Inventive Problem Solving (TRIZ) and suggests its utilization particularly within strategic management decision-making. TRIZ has widely been used especially in technical problem solving.

To illustrate TRIZ relevance, the Theory's 40 Principles of Inventive Problem Solving is applied in subsequent pages to issues related to strategy formulation, execution, and evaluation. Like any other creative approach, TRIZ requires that (i) the problem at hand be well defined and structured and (ii) then carefully analyzed. Among the companies that have utilized TRIZ are Avon, Caterpillar, DuPont, Fujitsu, IBM, Intel, Jonson & Johnson, Pfizer, Motorola, Siemens, and Toyota.

What is TRIZ?

Pronounced "treez," TRIZ is a Russian acronym that stands for the English acronym TIPS which in turn stands for "Theory of Inventive Problem Solving." Genrich Altshuller (1926-1998), a Russian inventor and author, is the originator of TRIZ. He and his colleagues embarked on an extensive, long-term, research project in the former Soviet Union on the subject of creativity. It is believed that the research work involved the analysis of millions of patents that were granted worldwide. The aim of the analysis was to discover how inventors arrived at solutions for technical/physical problems they encountered in their inventions. The analysis would have been considered a project concerning creative thinking and strategic problem solving.

According to the Altshuller Institute for TRIZ Studies, TRIZ is a methodology based on empirical data that can provide solution concepts for a wide variety of problems. Authors Barry, Domb, and Slocum capture the core of TRIZ by saying that somebody, somewhere, has already solved the problem you are dealing with, or have solved a very similar problem. Creativity, therefore, is to find that solution and adopt it. As a methodology (and body of knowledge), the influence of TRIZ is growing rapidly. This is partly because of its effectiveness in problem solving, partly because of continued research on the subject, and partly because of its application in various fields, including engineering, education, and management.

TRIZ Components

TRIZ methodology consists of concepts and methods that serve the purpose of creative decision-making and strategic thinking. Souchkov (2007) lists 24 TRIZ key components that include:

- Ideality
- Ideal Final Result
- Contradictions
- 40 Inventive Principles for Resolving Technical Contradictions
- Principles of Physical Contradiction Elimination
- 76 Inventive Standards
- The Theory of Technical Systems Development
- Laws and Trends of Technology Development
- Substance- Field Analysis
- Algorithm of Solving Inventive Problems (ARIZ)
- Subversion Analysis
- Trimming
- Alternative System Merging
- Creative Imagination Development Techniques
- Evaluation Techniques.

Decision-Making

Managing a business firm invariably involves decision-making, and managerial decisions must be made regardless of the firm's size, industry, or market position. The decisions seek to resolve key problems that the firm encounters. Effective decisions are intended to direct organizational resources towards the best possible allocation to achieve a sustainable competitive advantage. This is primarily the function of strategic decision-making.

Within the TRIZ construct, problems indicate the existence of contradictions or conflicts. Strategic decisions, therefore, are intended to eliminate the firm's contradictions. Many techniques for managerial decision-making have been introduced in recent decades. They include Brainstorming, Synectics, Neurolinguistic Programming, Lateral Thinking, Mind Machines, Mind Mapping, Forced Analogy, and Morphological Analysis. TRIZ is a powerful methodology to be added to problem solving toolkit because it is rooted in scientific analysis.

As is well publicized in the strategic management literature, decisions concerning strategy formulation, execution, and evaluation are different from routine, day-to-day managerial decisions. While routine decisions deal with tactical issues of the firm, strategic decisions are concerned with the firm's fundamental aspects of survival and growth. This does not mean that routine decisions are trivial or unimportant.

On the contrary, these decisions are relevant because they support the firm's operations and, thus, its strategic initiatives. The issue at hand is that routine decisions can be programmed on the basis of the firm's policies, procedures, directives, and practices. But strategic decisions are difficult, if not impossible, to be programmed while at the same time maintaining their usefulness. Strategic decisions, however, can be guided by scientific principles drawn from such fields as engineering and technology, as is the case with TRIZ methodology. Relying on a scientific approach is a normal practice in business disciplines. Fredrick Taylor, for example, pioneered Scientific Management by applying what he called "scientific methods" to improve workforce productivity and increase its output.

Ideal Final Result

An interesting model in TRIZ is the Ideal Final Result (IFR). It is defined as the most desired (or optimal) outcome to be reached for a problem or system under analysis. The IFR is visualized with the help of an equation that relates total benefits derived from solving a problem to the total possible adverse effects plus the cost of fixing the problem, as follows:

$$\frac{\text{total benefits}}{\text{total adverse effects} + \text{total anticipated cost}}$$

This relationship is the embodiment of a concept called Ideality, that is, a theoretical construct in which benefits begin to accelerate while, at the same time, the adverse effects and costs begin to decelerate, with the end result of achieving full benefits from the system in question. Ideality has become an important frame of reference for innovative problem solving. Its advantages are many including the following:

- It stimulates strategic thinking in problem solving.
- It leads to continuous systems improvement.
- It encourages the problem solver to seek an optimal solution for the problem at hand, rather than a sub-optimal one (i.e., the best solution vs. a good-enough one).
- It leads to efficient resource allocation.

Examples of IFR in strategic management include the following:

- Attaining continuous improvement in strategic initiatives at decreasing cost (e.g., time, efforts, resources, people).
- Identifying strategic alternatives at decreasing cost in the long-term.
- Implementing strategies (e.g., market development, strategic alliances) at lower cost and/or diminishing adverse effects.
- Achieving efficient resource allocation among competing uses without dislocation or operational disruption.

- Reaching consensus on strategic issues among management team members without harmful conflicts or resistance to change.

Problem Types

A distinction is made in TRIZ literature between three sets of problems: (i) technical problems, (ii) physical problems, and (iii) administrative problems. This classification is useful in crafting strategies because organizations face the same types of problems. The analysis of technical and physical problems occupies the central stage in TRIZ. This is due to the fact that the great majority of problems studied by Altshuller and his colleagues were of an engineering and technological nature.

The distinction between technical and physical problems is for analytical purposes; In some cases, an issue can be viewed as being both a technical as well as physical problem. The techniques utilized in solving technical problems, however, differ from those employed in dealing with physical problems.

TRIZ recognizes problems in terms of contradictions or conflicts within a system or within its components. That is to say that a problem is thought to be an embodiment of contradictions, and the creative elimination of the contradictions can automatically lead to the removal of the problem at hand. Solutions that involve trade-offs or compromises are rejected by TRIZ.

The reason is that such solutions are deemed uncreative and therefore unable to eliminate problems entirely. Rejection of trade-offs poses a dilemma for decision makers in utilizing TRIZ. For example, compromises are believed to be necessary in managing human resources to avoid major conflicts in the organization.

Technical problems

A technical problem exists if an improvement in a system or its components causes deterioration in other parts of the system. Business examples include the following:

- Increasing the visibility of a brand (positive outcome) demands a higher level of promotional expenditure (negative outcome).

- Enhancing the competitive advantage of a firm (positive outcome) requires additional resources (negative outcome).
- Improving the quality of a product (positive outcome) leads to higher production cost (negative outcome).
- Hiring qualified personnel (positive outcome) demands an extended search time (negative outcome).

Physical problems

A physical problem exists if opposing requirements or conditions are simultaneously placed on a system or its components. Business examples include the following:

- A smaller sales force required to achieve higher sales revenue.
- An in-depth situational analysis is to be performed with less resource commitment.
- Fewer company policies with greater impact on employees' behavior.
- Viable global marketing planning with shorter formulation and execution time.

Administrative problems

In an organizational setting, administrative problems are those that involve resource allocation among competing needs as well as managerial decisions concerning project design, staffing, execution, and delivery. Specifically, administrative problems include capital, technology, and labor. It also includes managerial attitudes, policies, and procedures. Administrative problems can impede innovative decision-making. TRIZ does not provide specific techniques for dealing with administrative problems.

More on the Physical Problems

As pointed out earlier, a physical problem (i.e., contradiction, conflict) exists if opposing demands are simultaneously imposed on a system or its components. For example, for a given laptop computer size, a lighter, but more powerful laptop, is desired. Another example is that a CEO decides on a substantial salary increase for employees while, at the same time, promises to deliver improved financial results for his company by the end of the following year.

Experts point out that Altshuller proposed 11 methods to resolve physical contradiction, including the following with business examples for illustration purposes:

- Separating the contradicting properties in space (e.g., divide a team with conflicting viewpoints into two teams).
- Separating the contradicting properties in time (e.g., extend a work shift into two or more shifts).
- The joining of homogenous and/or heterogeneous systems or elements into a super-system (e.g., integrate two or more work units/departments into one).
- A transition to a system that operates at a micro-level (e.g., divide a work unit/a department into two or more units).

Principles and Attributes

Altshuller introduced 40 Principles known as the Principles of Inventive Problem Solving. The purpose of the principles is to assist engineers, inventors, and others in their efforts to solve technical problems associated with man-made systems. The belief is that solving a system's technical problem will help improve its performance, and eventually lead the system to its IFR.

For example, an attempt to increase the capability of a bicycle to be driven faster is regarded as a technical problem, because increasing the speed may require changing the size of the wheels. This means that a conflict exists between the desired speed and the existing size of the wheels. A faster bicycle means in this case improved system performance.

Likewise, the desire to increase the productivity of a firm's employees can be considered an attempt to solve a technical problem because the level of expertise of the employees might not be compatible with the need to increase their productivity. Solving this problem (i.e., productivity increase) is expected, everything else being the same, to lead to a higher level of output.

The 40 Principles of Inventive Problem Solving were termed as such because of the belief in their ability to help solve challenging technical problem in a variety of situations. In seeking a solution for a technical problem, an individual can utilize one or more of the principles. Moreover, the Principles can also be utilized in conjunction with a set of 39 systems attributes or parameters developed by Altshuller. A problem solution can be arrived at by means of a format called the Contradiction Matrix.

In the Matrix, the 39 systems attributes are listed horizontally and vertically. And for each pair of different attributes, one or more of the 40 Principles are listed in the Matrix to indicate the most probable solution for the problem at hand. The benefits of the Contradiction Matrix are many and include the following:

- It is a convenient technique for finding solutions to technical problems.
- It speeds up the process of finding relevant solutions.
- It helps the business firm reduce the cost associated with finding solutions.
- It helps the firm with introducing new products or improving existing products.
- It supports the development of creative thinking for those who utilize it.
- It contributes to the sustainable competitive advantage of the firm.

The creation of an operationally reliable Contradiction Matrix can provide tremendous advantages to strategists. As is the case with Altshuller's Contradiction Matrix, the strategic management matrix will require the development of Principles as well as Parameters. The task is daunting because the matrix must be constructed on the basis of (i) Strategic Principles, and (ii) Strategic Parameters.

These two matrix pillars must be created on the basis of effective strategies of a very large number of successful firms, as is the case for Altshuller's Contradiction Matrix, which was constructed on the basis of examining millions of inventions. In addition, the Principles and the Parameters should be in the form of universality. That is to say that they should be relevant to firms that operate in various sectors of the economy.

Finally, the matrix needs to be constructed by taking into consideration all possible business strategies under different market structures (perfect competition, monopolistic competition, duopoly, oligopoly, and monopoly). Until such a Matrix can be constructed, Altshuller's 40 Principles as applied to strategic management can be utilized.

The Relevance of Nontechnical Applications

Although Altshuller and his colleagues advanced TRIZ primarily for utilization in the engineering field, there is no doubt that this methodology can be employed in other disciplines including strategic management. The deployment of TRIZ in other fields requires proper redesign of its Parameters to fit the nature of the specific disciplines under study.

For example, the parameters of strategic management may be different from those of marketing, and these, in turn, may be different from those of human resource management, and so on. Parameters are needed to build a Contradiction Matrix for each target discipline of interest. Of course, this need becomes critical if one believes that the 40 Principles (or their equivalents) are relevant for the discipline under discussion.

40 Inventive Principles for Strategic Management

The following are suggested applications, in the context of Altshuller's 40 Principles, in strategic management. The applications are meant to illustrate the relevance of the principles in the strategic management field under consideration.

Principle 1: *Segmentation* (Divide an object into independent parts)

- Divide strategic goals into objectives; divide objectives into tasks; and divide tasks into specific activities.

- Divide a grand strategy (e.g., diversification) into sub-strategies (e.g., concentric strategy); and divide a sub-strategy into sequential strategic initiatives.

- Share a strategy with an intended party as an aggregate whole and as disassembled individual components.

- Assign the requirements of strategy execution to divisions, departments, units, groups, and individuals.

- Break-down the aggregate benefits of a strategy formulation and execution in terms of financial return, market share, product/service development, skills enhancement, competency in technology, and company competitive advantage.

Principle 2: Extraction/Taking Out (Remove a disturbing part or property from an object)

- Single out desirable courses of action or initiatives.

- Identify the most unlikely obstacles in strategy implementation.

- Eliminate unimportant or impractical goals or objectives.

- Single out a unique business opportunity.

- Separate facts from emotions in decision-making and take out the latter.

Principle 3: Local Quality (Have different parts of an object carry out different functions)

- Make each of the 4Ps mix (product, price, place, and promotion) flexible enough to suite different target markets.

- Adopt strategies to fit local conditions (e.g., economic, legal) in different countries.

- Utilize an appropriate technology for each product or service offered.

- Design professional development programs in accordance with stages of strategic management process (strategy formulation, implementation, and evaluation).

- Ask each functional unit to show its contribution to the company's profitability.

Principle 4 Asymmetry (Replace a symmetrical form with an asymmetrical form of an object)

- Guide strategic initiatives toward the most promising product or service within a family of products or services.

- Of the company cultural value system, nurture two or three beliefs.

- Exert extraordinary efforts to promote a product or service in an attractive market.

- Assign teams with asymmetrical levels of authority to perform different tasks.

- Allocate a disproportionate number of resources to newly introduced products or services.

Principle 5: Combining/Integrating (Combine homogeneous objects or operations)

- Seek a forward integration strategy by establishing outlets to reach final customers.

- Adopt a horizontal integration strategy by acquiring a competitor at a bargain price.

- Implement a backward integration strategy by acquiring sources of inputs (e.g., raw material, components).

- Centralize workflows/operations in strategic locations.

- Create teams with different talents.

Principle 6: Universality (Have the object perform multiple functions)

- Implement multi-faceted strategies in large markets.

- Diversify product or service offerings.

- Seek a range of potential customers.

- Search for different sources of supplies, lenders, and employees.

- Hunt for local, national, and international market opportunities.

Principle 7: Nesting (Contain an object inside another which, in turn, is placed inside a third object)

- Create the organization's mission in light of its vision; goals in light of its mission; and objectives in light of its goals.

- Let business strategies follow corporate strategy; functional strategies follow business strategies; and operational strategies follow functional strategies.

- Design short-term plans on the basis of intermediate plans; and intermediate plans on the basis of long-term plans.

- Follow the pyramid model in budgetary resource allocation: fewer resources for smaller markets and greater resources for larger markets.

- Build a hierarchy of competencies: unit competency, departmental competency, divisional competency, and organizational competency.

Principle 8: Counterweight (Compensate for an object weight by joining with another object that has a lifting force)

- Make a functional strategy (e.g., new product introduction) contingent on the success of another functional strategy (e.g., market development).

- Design a "going global" strategy as a result of success in the domestic market.

- Build a line of products or services around an exceptionally demanded product or service.

- Create a mentoring program for new hires.

- Develop competencies in several areas of the business.

Principle 9: Prior Counteraction (If it is necessary to carry out some action, consider a counteraction in advance)

- Assess the drawback of current strategies.

- Evaluate the impact on the company's financial position of potential loses of an important customer.

- Estimate the effect of probable adverse economic conditions on the company's sales revenue.

- Figure out the cost of labor strike.

- Estimate the harm to the company as a result of "cutthroat" competition.

Principle 10: Prior Action (Carry out the required action in advance)

- Develop contingency strategic plans.

- Offer additional products or services.

- Target different markets.

- Find alternative or competing sources of funds, supplies, and distribution methods.

- Use different processes or technologies.

Principle 11: Cushion in Advance (Compensate for the low reliability of an object by a countermeasure taken in advance)

- Assemble beforehand a crisis and risk management team.

- Take precautionary steps prior to implementing an aggressive strategy such as a guerilla offensive.

- Initiate a thorough strategy evaluation prior to implementation.

- Adopt a strategic alliances strategy in undertaking major projects.

- Implement a preemptive strike strategy to secure lucrative markets or large customers.

Principle 12: Equipotentiality (Change the condition of work so that an object need not be raised or lowered)

- Utilize alternative methods (e.g., the Internet) as vehicles to convey the company's strategic initiatives to units, departments, divisions, and subsidiaries.

- Make it easy for managers to access necessary resources (e.g., personnel, software) for the purpose of strategy implementation.

- Provide real-time information about the strategy implementation progress.

- Facilitate communication between the company and its constituencies (e.g., employees, suppliers, investors).

- Take advantage of outsourcing arrangements to lower cost, enhance quality, and decrease the product or service price.

Principle 13: Inversion (Turn the object upside down)

- Build the company's capabilities during periods of economic slowdown.

- Expand the company's market share during a recession.

- Instead of adopting "follow the leader" strategy, let the leader follow you.

- Solicit feedback from employees about the company's performance.

- Change the company's structure from "tall" to "flat" or the other way around.

Principle 14: Spheroidicity (Replace linear parts with curved ones)

- Utilize a group of informed customers for strategy evaluation.

- Change the company's business strategy from offensive to defensive and vice versa during a drastic change in economic conditions.

- Establish company-owned outlets in some regions while franchising operations in other regions.

- Consider an alternative organizational structure (e.g., functional, matrix).

- Contemplate different kinds of managerial styles (e.g., open door policy, management by wandering around).

Principle 15: Dynamicity (Make characteristics of an object adjustable for optimal performance)

- Continuous review of strategy execution.

- Continuous monitoring of external developments.

- Daily review of the sales and financial position.

- Constant assessment of internal strengths and weaknesses.

- Steady screening of business opportunities.

Principle 16: Partial or Overdone Action (If it is difficult to obtain a desired effect with an action, then use more or less of the action)

- Pay special attention and allocate more resources to the execution of new strategic initiatives.

- Ignore the threat of weaker competitors.

- Eliminate or allocate minimum resources to marginal products.

- Put more emphasis on the implementation of objectives rather than goals.

- Stress the realization of the vision over the mission.

Principle 17: Moving to a New Dimension (Incline an object or turn it on the side)

- Expand market reach from local to regional; from regional to national; and from national to international.

- Adopt grander strategies.

- Move from a single business to a multi-business.

- Move from a competitive advantage to a sustainable competitive advantage.

- Acquire competitors.

Principle 18: Mechanical Vibration (Set an object into oscillation)

- Reenergize the company for quality, productivity, and innovative products or services with an incentive program.

- Let managers review strategic decisions prior to implementation.

- Create performance standards (e.g., balanced scorecard) for the company's units, departments, and the like.

- Challenge managers to meet or exceed exceptional performance standards.

- Carry out a large publicity program in the company's larger markets.

Principle 19: Periodic Action (Replace a continuous action with a periodic one)

- Conduct weekly or monthly reviews of the company's financial performance.

- Perform a bimonthly assessment of the company's strategic options.

- Carry out a quarterly analysis of the company's Competitive Strength Assessment (CSA).

- Conduct a quarterly analysis of the company's Five Forces Model.

- Assess, on a monthly basis, the company's vulnerability to external threats.

Principle 20: Continuity of Useful Action (Carry on an action without break)

- Continuous search for market opportunities.

- Constant utilization of successful strategies.

- Steady increase in market share.

- Relentless enhancement in organizational competencies.

- Persistent improvement of products and services.

Principle 21: Rushing Through (Perform a harmful operation at high speed)

- Carry out downsizing, if needed, rapidly

- Let strategic blunders teach management a fast lesson.

- Give top management a quick course in survival skills.

- Take swift actions to eliminate harmful conflicts.

- Quit a market as soon as feeling unable to compete.

Principle 22: Convert Harm into Benefit (Utilize a harmful factor to obtain a positive effect)

- Turn the intensity of rivalry into a motivating factor for gaining a competitive advantage.

- Let the resource shortage stimulate innovative approaches to organizational excellence.

- Establish challenging strategic goals to induce acceptable levels of performance.

- Forgo revenue for a period of time by making the company's products or services scarce.

- Learn survival lessons from more established competitors.

Principle 23: Feedback (Introduce feedback)

- Encourage employees to provide feedback on the company's strategies and policies.

- Obtain consumer feedback about the company's image, products, or services.

- Form a tiger team or hire a consulting firm to assess the company's overall position.

- Compare the firm's means of production (i.e., technology used) to that of the industry leader.

- Survey competitors' strengths and weaknesses using a competitive intelligence technique.

Principle 24: Intermediary (Use an intermediary object to carry out an action)

- Employ an agency to enhance the company's public image.

- Use the media to help the company achieve success.

- Transform the company into a virtual organization.

- Utilize mentor-protégé programs to gain additional business.

- Use loyal customers to prop-up the company's brand names.

Principle 25: Self-Service (Make the object service itself)

- Conduct a strategy audit to improve future strategic initiatives.

- Use balanced scorecard or other techniques to evaluate the company's overall performance.

- Expand the company's business domain through internally generated funds.

- Evaluate the company's situational analysis to eliminate its weaknesses.

- Review the company's CSA analysis to improve its market position.

Principle 26: Copying (Use an inexpensive copy instead of an object)

- Benchmark competitor best practices for learning purposes.

- Analyze other companies' strategies for "going global" and select a suitable one.

- Adopt a "follow the leader" approach in setting pricing strategies.

- Espouse the industry's standards in doing business.

- Target the same demographics as the closest competitors.

Principle 27: Use an Inexpensive Object Instead of an Expensive One (Replace an expensive object with a collection of inexpensive ones)

- Utilize temporary staff to collect and analyze industry and market information.

- Introduce cheaper products or services to meet the demand of low-income consumers.

- Contract-out company activities to lower cost providers.

- Select low-cost locations for company operations and distribution centers.

- Explore alternative cost-effective means of production.

Principle 28: Replacement of Mechanics Substitution (Use an electrical field to interact with an object)

- Hold strategy reviews and other top management meetings over the Internet.

- Utilize distance learning for professional development purposes.

- Explore alternative methods of producing goods or services.

- Experiment with different marketing techniques and strategies.

- Use new technologies (e.g., software) for product design and development.

Principle 29: Use of a Pneumatic Hydraulic Construction (Replace solid parts of an object with liquid)

- Keep lines of organizational communication open in all directions.

- Institute job rotation for senior executives.

- Streamline the company's organizational structure.

- Facilitate decision-making through delegation of authority.

- Build-up organizational competencies to achieve a sustainable competitive advantage.

Principle 30: Flexible Film of Membranes (Isolate an object from the outside environment)

- Show flexibility in executing strategies.

- Keep funds available for future expansion.

- Build a lean organizational structure.

- Avoid rigid rules and policies.

- Express adaptability in forming strategic alliances.

Principle 31: Use of Porous Materials (Make an object porous)

- Seek to create transparent relationships in the organization.

- Adopt an open-door policy as a managerial style.

- Explain new strategic initiatives to employees.

- Encourage interactions among different parts of the organization.

- Develop contingency plans to absorb the shocks of unwelcome events.

Principle 32: Changing the Color (Change the surrounding of an object or its color)

- Urge employees to support the company's vision.

- Serve different markets.

- Celebrate company successes and achievements.

- Add a new product or service line.

- Diversify the sources of supplies, funds, and demand.

Principle 33: Homogeneity (Make objects interact with a primary object)

- Make organizational policies harmonious.

- Seek congruency among vision, mission, goals, and objectives.

- Offer consistent quality of goods or services.

- Follow the same methodology in developing business strategies.

- Unite the organization's members around a vision.

Principle 34: Rejecting and Generating Parts (Restore any used-up parts of an object)

- Reenergize employees for commitment, productivity, and excellence.

- Cease operations in declining demand markets.

- Reemphasize periodically the organization's core values.

- Reengineer the organization's functions and processes.

- Review operations, procedures, instructions, and policies to eliminate redundancy.

Principle 35: Transformation of Physical or Chemical States of an Object (Change the aggregate state of an object)

- Transform some of the organization's units into virtual entities.

- Utilize the service of freelance contractors to accomplish organizational functions.

- Design lines of products or services to satisfy the demand of groups of customers.

- Seek the participation of employees in formulating strategies.

- Use consumers' "preference identification" technology to learn about potential changes in market demand.

Principle 36: Phase Transition (Implement an effect on the object)

- Design strategies for different phases of business cycles.

- Coach employees for changes in managerial leadership.

- Prepare the organization for going global.

- Train managers for impending joint ventures.

- Appoint a transformation leader.

Principle 37: Thermal Expansion (Use different materials)

- Employ moderately conservative to highly ambitious strategies in accordance with economic contraction or expansion.

- Encourage competition among teams.

- Increase spending on promotional campaigns during periods preceding national holidays.

- Offer market unique goods or services.

- Empower employees to help them realize self-actualization.

Principle 38: Use Strong Oxidizers (Replace normal air with enriched air)

- Espouse high ethical standards for the organization.

- Adapt challenging organizational goals.

- Strive for elevated levels of performance.

- Promote middle managers for executive positions.

- Initiate a plan for continuous organizational improvement.

Principle 39: Inert Environment (Replace the normal environment with an inert one)

- Implement de Bono's "Six Thinking Hats" approach in strategy sessions.

- Build a harmonious corporate environment.

- Encourage diversity of opinions in management meetings.

- Invite outside speakers to company meetings to shore-up creativity and excellence.

- Introduce periods of, or encourage employees to take part in, "creative thinking" exercises in the workplace.

Principle 40: Composite Material (Replace a homogenous material with a composite one)

- Utilize various sources of information in formulating strategies.

- Assemble a multidisciplinary taskforce to manage organizational crises.

- Let the human resources strategy diversify human capital and talents.

- Serve different markets; use different distribution channels; and implement a blend of sales methods.

- Build an organization with layers of security protection.Chapter Summary

Chapter Summary

The decision-making process of strategy formulation, execution, and evaluation can be enriched by augmenting its elements with practical and useful approaches. TRIZ is such an approach that has proven to be invaluable for practitioners and academicians in engineering and other technical fields. It has also been utilized in recent years in nontechnical areas such as education.

TRIZ, in its bare essential, can be viewed as a method for creative decision-making and strategic thinking. In the broader perspective, it is a body of knowledge that consists of tools, techniques, and perspectives designed to achieve technological progress by helping individuals tackle difficult problems and deliver optimal solutions.

TRIZ can be applied to the strategic management process (as well as to other business administration disciplines) by utilizing some of its techniques, including the 40 Principles of Inventive Problem Solving, the Contradiction Matrix, and the Ideal Final Result. In this chapter we explored some of TRIZ's techniques and attempted to translate the 40 Principles into applications in strategic management. The deployment of TRIZ in strategic management is an area that deserves further research and practice.

Chapter Questions

1. What is the difference between TRIZ and SWOT?
2. Can TRIZ be used for product invention?
3. What is meant by the ideal final result?
4. Would you consider TRIZ as an artificial intelligence technology? Explain.
5. Should TRIZ be deployed in managerial planning? Explain.

Chapter 13

Entrepreneurial Mindset of Immigrants in the United States: Venture and Job Creation

"I am the daughter of refugees. The immigrant's mentality is to work hard, be brave, and never give up in your pursuit of achieving the American dream."

Reshma Saujani

Learning Objectives:

- Grasp the diversity and cultural background of immigrants.
- Discover the contributions of immigrants to the U.S. economy.
- Recognize tendency of immigrants for venture creation.
- Learn about job creation of immigrants' businesses.

The United States has long been a favorite destination of people from around the world whose motivation is to settle in and contribute talents to the economic and technological progress of the adopting country. Data show that immigrants are an important source of workforce supply, job creation, and venture development. The purpose of this chapter is twofold: (i) to review immigration trends in the country in recent years to learn about its magnitude relative to global trends, and (ii) provide an initial estimation of immigrants' contribution to venture creation and employment in the country.

Global Migration

The movement of people across national borders to settle in a desired land is a phenomenon that goes back to early human civilization. This movement is generally governed by forces beyond the influence of individuals to dictate. According to a 2020 report about global migration titled "Peace, Dignity, and Equality on a Healthy Planet," the United Nations classified the reasons that force people to migrate into the following:

- Search for work.
- Quest for economic opportunity.
- Join family members.
- Study abroad.
- Internal country conflict.
- Escape persecution or human rights violation.
- Natural disasters.

According to the 2020 World Migration Report, the number of international migrants was estimated at 272 million in 2019 as compared to 84 million in 1970, an increase of about 224 percent. The movement of people across national borders as immigrants has far-reaching impacts upon the countries of destination. This impact goes far beyond that of increased workforce supply, business creation, elevated levels of productivity, and greater economic growth. In the long-run immigrants can also affect the social, political, and technological environment of their adopted countries. The Organization for Economic Cooperation and Development (OECD) published a study in 2014 titled "Migration Policy Debates" in which it classified the impact of immigrants on host countries into three major categories: (i) labor markets, (ii) public policy, and (iii) economic growth. Briefly, the study indicated the following:

- Immigrants accounted for 47 percent of the increase in the workforce in the US and 70 percent in Europe over a period of ten years.

- They contribute more to taxes and social contributions than they receive in benefits.
- They contribute to technological progress.
- They arrive to the countries of destination with skills.
- They contribute to capital development of the host countries.

U.S. Immigration

The U.S. has long been a favorite destination of people from around the world. The intensity of immigrant inflow into the country is largely influenced by conflicts and economic circumstances in other countries. Recent examples include immigration from Ukraine, Ethiopia, Afghanistan, Peru, Venezuela, and Mexico. The number of immigrants to the country increased from 595,014 in 1981 to 1,031,765 in 2019, a jump of 73 percent. In 2019, the U.S hosted about one percent of global migration. Table 1 illustrates the world's regions from which U.S. immigrants originated in 2019.

Table 1

U.S. Immigration by Region, 2019

Region	Number of Immigrants	Percent of Total Immigrants (%)
Asia	352,593	34.2
South and Central America	149,109	14.5
Caribbean	135,605	13.1
Africa	110,048	10.7
Europe	90,810	8.9
Sub-total	878,263	85.1
Mexico	153,502	14.9
Total	1,031,765	100.0

Source: Yearbook of Immigration Statistics, 2019, Department of Home Security.

It is interesting to note that, in 2019, more than 50 percent of U.S. immigrants were originated in 16 countries (Table 3). The majority of them (14.9 percent of the total) came from Mexico, followed by China (5.8 percent), and Indian (5.0 percent). As expected, the great majority of immigrants were originated from developing countries that are members of the 193 United Nations countries.

Table 2

Selected U.S. Immigration by Country of Last Residence, 2019

Country	Number of Immigrants	Percent of Total Immigrants (%)
Mexico	153,502	14.9
China	60,029	5.8
India	51,139	5.0
Philippines	43,478	4.2
Vietnam	38,944	3.8
El Salvador	24,326	2.4
Brazil	19,607	1.9
Colombia	18,715	1.8
Korea	18,120	1.8
Haiti	16,991	1.6
Honduras	15,543	1.5
Venezuela	15,150	1.5
Guatemala	13,111	1.3
Ecuador	11,189	1.1
Egypt	10,415	1.0
Ethiopia	10,109	1.0
Total	**520,368**	**50.4**

Source: Yearbook of Immigration Statistics, 2019, Department of Home Security.

Entrepreneurial Tendency of Immigrants

Government agencies, international organizations, and scholars have discussed international migration and its effects on global and national economies. Immigration policies differ among countries and perceptions about its consequences vary among the interested parties.

The issue of immigration and self-employment has especially attracted the attention of many authors in recent years. For instance, Fisher and Lewin (2018), in a study about Hispanic self-employment in the United States, concluded that there are two key factors that draw Hispanics to entrepreneurial activities:

- The incentive to earn more income than being employed by others.
- Limited available employment opportunities for immigrants.

The Pew Research Center reported that the majority of Latinos say skin color impacts business opportunities in the United States. For example, 62 percent of the 3,375 adult Hispanic who were surveyed in 2021 believe that darker skin color hurts their ability to get ahead in the workplace. On the other hand, Alaslani and Collins (2017) attributed the motivation of Muslims in Sydney, Australia for self-employment to racial discrimination in the labor market.

Azoulay et al (2020) pointed out that immigrants in the United States act more as job creators in the country than job takers, and that non-U.S. born business founders play a greater role in U.S. entrepreneurial growth of high-technology firms. In discussing the contribution of high-skilled immigrants to the technological advancement, Bernstein et al (2018) pointed out that immigrants are responsible for 30 percent of U.S. innovation and that their indirect spillover accounts for more than twice their direct productivity contribution.

In a multi-country study, Brieger and Gielnik (2021) concluded that female immigrants, as compared to their male counterparts, are less likely to start and run their own business in host countries. According to Skandalis and Ghazzawi (2014), the main factor that influences immigrants to become entrepreneurs is the need for economic advancement. Awotoye and Singh (2018) believe that, even though immigrants experience higher level of stress, they continue to maintain an elevated level of intention to establish business firms than non-immigrants.

Vandor (2021) believes that the reason immigrants are more likely than the native population to become entrepreneurs is because of their propensity for risk-taking in the business field.

Xu et al (2019) studied a sample of Chinese entrepreneurs and found out that the success of the entrepreneurs can be attributed to their psychological adaptation (e.g., positive mindset, emotion management) and socio-cultural adaptation (e.g., language skills, cultural learning). Krichevskiy et al (2016) asserted that U.S. immigrants arriving from economically advanced countries are more likely than others to engage in entrepreneurial activities in the country.

Finally, Sundararajan and Sundararajan (2015) asserted that immigrants' prior entrepreneurial experience and knowledge enable them to better recognize business opportunities in host countries as compared to non-immigrant entrepreneurs.

Assessing the Contributions of Immigrants

USA Facts database estimated that the immigrant population in the United States was at 44.93 million in 2019, or 13.7 percent of total population. Based on this data and the assumptions listed below, we estimate the immigrants' new business creation and consequently, employment generation for the period 2011-2019.

The estimation while preliminary, is desirable because of (i) scarcity of scholarly research on the impact of new arrivals of immigrants on the national economy, and (ii) the relevance of the findings to the country's immigration policy. To estimate the contributions of immigrants to the U.S. economy, we postulate the following:

- Newly arriving immigrants to the United States have the same entrepreneurial tendency to launch business ventures as that of the general population.
- Newly arriving immigrants initiate 13.7 percent of the newly

established business firms as well as employment, a ratio that reflects the share of immigrants in the total population in the country.

- All immigrants have the same or very similar entrepreneurial mindset regardless of their country of origin.

Table 3 shows the estimated share of venture creation and employment of new arrivals of immigrants in the United States for the period 2011-2019.

Table 4

Births and Employment of New Business Establishments
(In thousands)

Year	Births of establishments	Estimated Immigrants' Share *	Employment	Estimated Immigrants' Share*
2011	834	114	3,076	421
2012	881	121	3,199	438
2013	861	118	3,158	433
2014	890	122	3,251	445
2015	957	131	3,429	470
2016	953	131	3,064	420
2017	971	133	3,352	459
2018	1,031	141	3,113	427
2019	1,036	142	3,410	467

Source of raw data: U.S. Bureau of Labor Statistics, https://www.bls.gov/news.release/cewbd.t08.htm
*13.7 percent of total.

As the table shows, immigrants created 142,000 businesses in 2019 as compared to 114,000 in 2011, an increase of 25 percent. They also added 467,000 jobs in 2019 as compared to 421,000 jobs in 2011, an increase of 11 percent. Undoubtedly, international migration has far-reaching effects (positive and negative) in the long-term on the global economy as well as individual host countries.

Chapter Summary

People are motivated differently to move across national borders to settle in desired host countries. Some migrate in search of economic opportunities, others seek security, still others strive for religious freedom. Whatever the motivation for the movement, immigrants, like the rest of people in host countries, will end up consumers (demanders), producers (suppliers), and owners (employers). Research findings suggest that immigrants generate large economic benefits to host countries' economies (e.g., Murphy 2017; Chakravorty, 2019; Zhu and Pulleyblank, 2020).

The United States is known as the "nation of nations." The country has been since its inception the destination of immigrants from all corners of the world who contribute their labor, skills, and ingenuity to fostering the nation's economy and strengthening its competitive advantage. This chapter explored the flow of U.S. immigrants in recent years to understand their contribution to venture creation and employment.

Chapter Questions

1. What are some of the contributions of immigrants to the United States?
2. What are the costs of immigration to recipient countries? To the originating countries?
3. Do you think that the inflow of immigrants into the U.S. accelerates the countries technological and competitive advantage?
4. As a business consultant to recent immigrants, what would you recommend them to do?
5. Is entrepreneurship a global phenomenon? Explain.

Chapter 14

Forces Influencing the Performance of U.S. Family-Owned Businesses

"I went into family business. To me, it was the norm and not the exception."

Tyne Daly

Learning Objectives:

- Learn about family businesses in the United States.
- Understand the factors that influence the growth of family businesses.
- Recognize the diversity of family businesses.
- Grasp the importance of family businesses to the economy.

Family-owned business firms are the world's oldest form of commercial enterprises. The firms symbolize national pride in many countries, act as the sole provider of income for millions of families, and the source of entrepreneurial risk-taking and opportunity-seeking for generations of family members. This chapter discusses the landscape of family business in the US and the factors that influence the firms' performance and, hence, increase the chances of their longevity and growth.

The discussion is guided by two scholarly views of the firm's sustainable competitive advantage rooted in strategic management literature: (i) the resource-based view, and (ii) the industrial organization view. Key factors addressed include family cohesiveness, vision, innovation, community affiliation, and government support. The chapter may also provide an interesting learning experience for would-be entrepreneurs who may be planning to start a family-owned business.

A Brief Historical Background

Willium O Hara observed (the Siliconindia, 2014) that "Before the multinational corporation, there was family business. Before the industrial revolution, there was family business. Before the enlightenment of Greece and the empire of Rome, there was family business." Indeed, the history of family-owned firms dates to many centuries ago. For example, according to the Family Business Magazine (2015), the oldest family-owned business in Japan is Kongo Gumi, a construction enterprise that was establish in 578, followed in the year 718 by another Japanese firm, Innkeeping Hoshi Ryokan.

In the United Stated, the oldest family-owned businesses are Follett, Gilbane, and Kohler, which all were founded in 1873 (Forbes, 2011). Family-owned businesses are fascinating for their diversity, universality, accessibility, and contribution to national economies. They are found in many sectors and industries in every country and region of the world. The businesses differ in size, innovativeness, ownership structure, leadership vision, and strategies. Some of them are globally oriented while others are domestically- or locally focused. Some of them are highly competitive while others are on the verge of bankruptcy or already disappeared. In brief, family-owned firms are a unique kind of commercial entities that deserve policymakers' attention to help boost their viability, growth, and competitive advantage.

It is suggested (e.g., Liu et al, 2012) that the theoretical perspectives of family-owned firms' performance have been dominated by traditional theories such as the resource-based view and agency theory. It appears that traditional approaches to the subject matter are inadequate and, therefore, more innovative inquiries are needed.

This chapter proposes a broader set of essential factors to the discussion, namely, the two views constructed to theorize the performance determinants of family-owned firms and, thus, the likelihood of their survival and growth. The proposed construct is inspired by two theoretical approaches that influence the firm's performance: (i) the resource-based view and (ii) the industrial organization view[34].

Family Business Research

Family-owned businesses in the United States and elsewhere around the world have been the subject of research (e.g., Rosa, 2009; Visser and van Scheers, 2018; Vrontis et al, 2019; LIanos-Contreras and Jabri, 2019; Wu et al, 2020) because, among other things, as Chami (2001, p.3), argued, "Family businesses have played a key role in modernization of the developed and developing countries.

The family's ability to provide the crucial capital and entrepreneurial spirit is deemed crucial to the development of capitalism and in spurring the industrialization of the developed countries." The Conway Center for Family Business stated that family-owned firms in the United States are the backbone of the country's economy and that the greatest part of the national wealth lies with these organizations. Moreover, Pieper et al, (2021, p.2), emphasized that "Family businesses are key pillars of the U.S. economy and essential to economic and societal prosperity."

A family-owned business, as a commercial enterprise, can be small, mid-sized, or large. The majority of them worldwide appear to be micro firms (employing less than 20 individuals each). Astrachan and Shanker (2003) defined the term family business by deploying two criteria: (i) family participation in the management of the business regardless of its size or activity domain, and (ii) family control of the

---

34   In essence, the resource-based view postulates that the firm's performance is more influenced by its internal resources than by external factors, while the industrial organization view asserts that external (industry) factors are more important than the internal ones in deciding the firm's competitive advantage and, hence, performance (e.g., David Fred R. and David, Forest R. (2017, pp. 63 and 93). *Strategic Management*, Boston: Massachusetts, Pearson Education, Inc).

business strategic direction. Authors have investigated family business from different perspectives. For example, Riordan and Riordan (1993), discussed family norms that include the following attributes:

- Family business provides income opportunity to needy relatives.
- The business does not differentiate among siblings.
- The business is an important source of on-the-job training and skills development for immediate or extended family members.

Moreover, according to mybusiness.com., the advantages of a family-owned business include:

- Unified business leadership and commitment of family members.
- Stability of the business.
- Trust and authenticity among members.
- Role flexibility and versatility of the members.
- Emphasis on long-term goals and the business vision.
- Inclusion in the business of next-generation family members.

Simon and Hitt (2003) pointed out that family-owned firms, as unique organizations, enjoy the following attributes:

- Human capital - skills, knowledge, and other individual's competencies.
- Social capital - relationship among individuals or organizations.
- Patient capital - invested financial capital without the threat of liquidation,
- Governance structure - lower governance cost that could be the source of the firm's competitive advantage.
- Survivability capital - pooled family resources available to the firm.

Penney et al (2019) reported that published research implies that the family business often pursues risky or aggressive strategies despite the common wisdom to preserve socioemotional wealth, that is, conservativism in family business decisions. Zou et al (2014), in analyzing family-owned firms found out that the firms' operating efficiency is less efficient than non-family firms. The author attributed the difference to the ownership structure and management of the businesses. In a study about European business firms, Fröhlich (1991) observed that the firms are inwardly looking closed systems, that their strategic behavior is conservative, and that they are far from being dynamic factors of the economy.

On the other hand, Hoffman, James et al (2006) believe that high-level family capital has a powerful impact on family-owned business performance; it also holds a sustainable competitive advantage over low-level nonfamily businesses.

In terms of business performance, Abdelgawad and Zahra (2020) discussed the concept of spiritual capital (i.e., religious values and beliefs) held by some families of family-owned firms that influence the firms' strategic direction and distinguishes their firms from others. Tabor et al (2020) postulated that spiritual leadership in family-owned firms serves as a resource to increase employees' commitments. Brundin et al (2014) mentioned that the performance and other aspects of family businesses are influenced by ideas and norms of its corporate governance. Kula and Tatoglu (2006) found out that, in the context of Turkish family businesses, the firms' performance is positively related to the directors' attributes associated with access to information, effectiveness of board of directors, and observance of fiduciary responsibility.

Aloulou (2018), in a study about family businesses in Saudi Aribia, found out the performance of a family firm is influenced by the family involvement in the management of the business. Chirapanda (2020) discussed the critical success factors for Japanese family-owned firms which include innovation, competitive advantage, managerial leadership, and community relationships.

Leibell (2010) indicated that a McKinsey & Company Report entitled The Five Attributes of Ensuring Family Business emphasized five major activities that influence the performance of family businesses:

- Harmonious relations among family members.
- Ownership structure that provides sufficient capital for business growth.
- Strong governance of the company.

- Professional management of family's wealth.
- Charitable foundation to promote family values across generations.

More to the point, Craig et al (2008) declared that developing a family-based brand identity positively contributes to firm performance in terms of growth and profitability. A study by Kavas et al (2020) about some Islamic firms in Turkey concluded that religion plays an important role in shaping business activities in family-owned firms and, hence, performance. According to the authors, this is realized via three mechanisms: (i) family religious beliefs influence the way by which the business is conducted, (ii) family adheres to religious values as the basis for managing the business, (iii) family religious values define business taboos to evil eyes. Ramos, Maria et al (2011) asserted that the founder of a family-owned firm has a lasting influence on the firm including its culture, beliefs, and rules of conduct of its members.

Beehr et al (1997) indicated that family members of a small family firm typically experience conflicts related to business decisions. Suess-Reyes (2017) addressed the issue of governance in family business by saying that strengthening governance can foster communication in managing the enterprise and enhance individual members' emotional investment in the business. Jefferson et al (2020) stated that the perpetuation of entrepreneurial behavior in family-owned firms has been influenced by the family itself because the family is an institution that unites its members while, at the same time, guiding or restricting their choices. In a discussion about branding, Claudia and Botero (2018) asserted that family desires for branding is driven by its identity-related (e.g., pride) and outcome-related (e.g., reputation) motives.

Performance of Family Business

Scholars have approached the concept of theory from different angles. Swanson and Chermack (2013, p. 15), for example, pointed out that applied theories are "complete representations of systems activities." Gioia and Pure (1990, p. 587) viewed theory as "Any coherent description or explanation of observed or experienced phenomena." Torraco (2008, p. 115) indicated that "A theory simply explains what a phenomenon is and how it works." Finally, Kamasak et al (2017) regarded theory as a process of building a statement of concepts that shows how and/or why a phenomenon occurs.

In highlighting the significance of theory construction, Robison et al (2021) pointed out that theories are needed to guide best practices. Rivard (2020, p.1) asserted that "the outcomes of a researcher's theorizing efforts are often incomplete explanations of a phenomenon, which…may develop into rich theories." Parsons (2017, p. 9) stated that "A theory in science is a logical creation…yet a scientific theory doesn't necessarily represent absolute truth."

On the other hand, Wacker (1998) observed that theory-building is important because it: (i) provides a framework for analysis, (ii) supports efficient deployment of fields of knowledge, and (iii) enables real-world problem applications. The author added that good theories possess the attributes of abstraction, uniqueness, parsimony, internal consistency, and generalizability.

It is interesting to note that in the field of family scholarly studies, a wide range of theories have been advanced during past decades to address a variety of social or psychological aspects of the family as a social institution. For instance, research has investigated family communication pattern, value systems, health concerns, relationships, and so on. In general, the theories attempt to guide the family to best practices (e.g., education) or explain the family's behavioral pattern (e.g., affection) among its members. Examples of the theories include:

- Behavioral change theory.
- Family equilibrium theory.
- Attachment theory.
- Family systems theory.
- Family socialization theory.
- Adaptation theory.
- Realist social theory.

On the other hand, Scholars have suggested several theories about family-owned business firms. The theories address different aspects of the firms including market performance, decision-making process, resources, ownership structure, growth prospects, and competitive advantage. As one might expect, variation of opinions and approaches exist even among authors who advocate the same construct. Among the notable theories are the following:

- Agency – A family-owned firm is postulated to be characterized by a set of agency relationships among its members (e.g., Van den Berghe and Carchon, 2003).
- Gender – The influence of family members' gender on such matters as decision-making of the family business, its gender performance, reinforcement, and strategy (e.g., Al-Dajani, Haya et al, 2014).
- Field – The theory is deployed to explain the creation of family-owned firm by stating that individual's choice to enter a family business venture is affected by situational factors (e.g., Kjellman (2014).
- Social Identity – The theory has been adopted to investigate factors that contribute to the development of family social capital (e.g., Schmidts and Shepherd, 2015).
- Resource – The theory has been employed as a framework to elaborate on the firm's internal resources and its competitive advantage (e.g., Habberston and Williams, 1999; Hansson, 2015).

The Two-Views Construct

This chapter introduces a theoretical perspective to explain key factors that influence the performance of the family-owned business firm. In developing the perspective, the following features of the firm are taken into consideration. The features are the ramifications for the firms' creation and, hence, its business activities.

- The firm provides the family with a stream of income and contributes to national income, employment, and technological advancement.
- It offers an employment opportunity to family-and other-related members.

- It supplies goods or services to the market.
- It preserves the family's name as well as fosters its reputation in the community.
- It is a conduit for the family, as the stakeholder, to discuss the introduction of innovative products or services, better technology, improved procedures, and managerial practices.
- It is a forum for the family to reach consensus about the firm's strategic decisions that influence the survival and growth of the business. Consensus decisions are believed to be a source for the firm's competitive advantage, in additional to the family combined individuals' resources.
- The firm's performance is subject to influence by the family's values, beliefs, cohesiveness, and other internal intangible and tangible assets. In line with the widely known Michael Porter's five forces model, the firm's performance is also affected by its industry environment, including market structure (e.g., perfect competition, duopoly), intensity of demand, and governmental support.

Chapter Summary

Family-owned businesses play a vital role in the United States. According to the Grand Valley State University (www.gvsu.edu), for example, these businesses contribute 57 percent of the country's Gross Domestic Product (GDP), employ 63 percent of the workforce, and employ 98 million persons. Moreover, A family-owned business, as a commercial enterprise, can be a small, mid-sized, or large firm. Most of them are small micro firms, each employing less than 20 individuals. Authors have advanced several theories to explain business performance of these businesses.

The explanations include: (i) religious values and beliefs, (ii) ideas and norms of its corporate governance, and (iii) the businesses' directors' access to information as well as observance of fiduciary responsibility to family members. Undoubtedly, the forces that influence the performance of business firms – regardless of their size or ownership structure – are many and diverse. In this chapter, the emphasis is placed on the firms' internal factors such as leadership and external factors such as the health of the national economy. We termed this approach to explain the performance as the two-views construct.

Chapter Questions

1. How would you define the term family-owned business?
2. Why do families own businesses? Discuss.
3. Are family businesses necessary for the U.S. economy? If so, explain.
4. What is theory? Why do you think that theories are deployed in the field of family business?
5. How would you manage a family business? Explain.

Chapter 15

The Road to Entrepreneurial Leadership

"Leadership is a way of thinking, a way of acting and, most importantly, a way of communicating."

Simon Sinek

Learning Objectives:

- Review leadership theories.
- Discover the relationship between leadership and entrepreneurship.
- Understand the nature of entrepreneurial leadership.
- Explore the importance of entrepreneurial leadership to business firms.

Scholars have for many decades attempted to answer the following questions: What is leadership? What makes a good leader? What are the ingredients of effective leadership? What are the leadership styles? Are leaders born or made? The purpose of this chapter is to address these inquiries by: (i) discussing the meaning of leadership, (ii) reviewing leadership theories, (iii) examining the relationship between entrepreneurship and leadership, and finally (iv) exploring entrepreneurial leadership as an emerging body of knowledge and as a leadership style for the twenty-first century of workplace inclusion, diversity, and equity.

Leadership is a captivating topic to study because leadership (or its absence) seems to be everywhere around us in private businesses, government agencies, educational institutions, and international organizations. Knowledge of leadership, its practices, its styles, and its theories can enable the individual to become an effective leader able to bring out the best technical and human qualities of his and her subordinates (or teams) to achieve the organization's strategic goals.

Leadership theories are diverse, informative, and inspiring. Some of the theories attempt to explain the personality attributes of leaders, some of them focus on the behavioral pattern of leaders, and some of them highlight the environmental circumstances that empower individuals to become leaders in business, government, politics, or the society at large.

What is Leadership?

Leadership is a phenomenon that goes back to early times of human existence, family formation, and group organization. Trends in leadership style and, hence, the definition of leadership, are greatly influenced by a host of cultural, economic, educational, psychological, and social factors. Northouse (2019), in a book titled "Leadership: Theory and Practice," reviewed the evolution of leadership definitions for the period from 1900 to early the 21st century. The author indicated, for instance, that at a conference on leadership in 1927, B.V. Moore defined leadership as "the ability to impress the will of the leader on those led and induce obedience, respect, loyalty, and cooperation." Northouse concluded that scholars for more than a century "can't come up with a common definition for leadership" (p.41). While Robbins (1993, p. 365), on the other hand, defined leadership as "The ability to influence a group toward the achievement of goals." Nelson and Quick (2006, p. 388) defined it as "The process of guiding and directing the behavior of people in the work environment."

In this book leadership is treated in the context of the business enterprise. No emphasis is placed, for example, on political or community leadership, although there is common ground among all kinds of leadership in a society. As the emphasis is on business leadership, we propose the following definition: *Leadership is a quality of the individual that inspires and motivates the behavior of others in the organization to exert utmost efforts for the purpose of achieving the organization's strategic goals.*

The qualities of the leader may be acquired from various sources such as genetics, specific learning, certain forming situations, or other sources. The situational aspect of leadership refers to an event that triggers its occurrence such as natural disaster or social upheaval. This is sometimes referred to as the heroic view of leadership. The leadership quality takes different forms called attributes or styles. The following is further elaboration on the definition mentioned above:

- In organizational settings leadership is a continuous process (i.e., a series of actions and activities) during an extended period of time.
- The leader's intent is to influence and motivate subordinates.
- The purpose of the influence and motivation is to achieve the organization's goals.
- The motivation can be in the form of financial or nonfinancial rewards.

Leadership Theories

Leadership is a complex human phenomenon like psychology or sociology. Thus, it requires study and analysis to grasp. To fully understand leadership, we will review some of the main theories of leadership.

The Great Man Theory[35]

---

35   See for example, Organ, Dennis W. (1996). Leadership: The Great Man Theory Revisited, *Business Horizon*, 39(3), 1-4. Stringham, Edward P (2017). Hamilton's Legacy and the Great Man Theory of Financial History, *The Independent Review*, 21(4), 523-533.

The Great Man Theory is one of the oldest leadership theories. The theory is illustrated by the saying that "great leaders are born and not made." The theory stipulates that some people unlike others are born to prominent leadership positions. Examples include emperors, kings, and tribal heads. Another related approach to leadership is called the "Situational Theory" in which case individuals emerge as spontaneous leaders in situations that critically demand their vision, talent, or stamina. As is the case with other leadership theories, the Great Man Theory has been debated in the literature on the basis that it offers incomplete treatment of leadership phenomenon in addition to the belief that leadership attributes can be learned.

Trait Theory

Trait theory is perhaps the most renowned approach in personality psychology in the field of leadership. The theory attempts to identify the primary characteristics of individuals. A trait is considered a relatively enduring quality for which an individual differs from others. The theory stipulates that leadership can be explained based on personality attributes of leaders, and that leaders possess certain attributes that are not shared with non-leaders.

For example, Thomas (2010, p.1) emphasized that the theory is associated with the axiom that "great leaders are born that way." An implication of the theory is that people, being different from each other, can be classified into groups on the basis of their inner characteristics. Recent years have witnessed several scholarly contributions to the theory as well as variations in the theoretical approaches to its development and acceptance.

Psychologists believe that personality can be understood by the fact that people possess certain behavioral traits or characteristics such as being shy, aggressive, optimistic, and so on. According to Shukla, Archana (https://udrc.lkouniv.ac.in) trait theory attempts to identify, analyze, and predict the primary attributes of individuals.

On the other hand, Yunus et al (2018) pointed out that personality can be observed from the individual's traits such as ways of thinking, behavior, and emotional response. The authors pointed out that scholars have recognized five core personality traits referred to as the Big Five Theory:

- Extraversion (e.g., sociable, energetic, enthusiastic).
- Agreeableness (e.g., cooperative, trusting, helpful).
- Conscientiousness (e.g., careful, responsible, well-organized).
- Neuroticism ((e.g., careful, well-organized).
- Openness (e.g., imaginative and having either great or narrow interests).

Moreover, Northouse (2019) mentioned that R. M. Stogdill[36] reviewed research findings of 287 publications for the period 1948 to 1974 about leadership characteristics and discovered that the publications came up with a variety of traits. The following is a selected sample of them:

- Persistence in goals achievement.
- Willingness to assume risk.
- Originality in problem solving.
- Initiatives orientation.
- Self-confidence.
- willingness to accept his/her decisions consequences.
- Readiness to deal with interpersonal stress.
- Frustration tolerance.
- Desire for task accomplishment.
- Ability to influence other people's behavior.

Behavioral Theory

The Behavioral Theory is a set of related theories and research findings. Behavioral theories emerged as a response to the deficiencies of trait theories because trait theories discuss leaders' attributes but don't explain how they behave. The theory promotes the thesis that leadership

---

36   Stogdill, R. M. (1948). Personal factors associated with leadership: A survey of the literature. Journal of Psychology, 25, 35–71. Stogdill, R. M. (1974). Handbook of leadership: A survey of theory and research. New York, NY: Free Press.

is not an innate capability of people and that individuals can be taught to become successful leaders (Uslu, 2019). The behavior of leaders is influenced by a range of factors including beliefs, emotions, attitudes, and the situation in which he/she encounters.

Moreover, leadership effectiveness depends on the leader's behavior in relation to his/her followers. In other words, individuals can be made leaders through education, learning, and training. Individuals are not born to assume leadership positions. Effective leadership is based on learnable behavior. This group of theories indicate that observable human behaviors differentiate leaders from non-leaders (Robbins, p. 368). Nelson and Quick (2006) indicated that there are four major schools of thought about behavioral leadership:

- The distinction between autocratic, democratic, and laissez-faire.
- Two dimensions to leadership: (a) initiating structure, and (b) consideration.
- Two leadership styles: (a) employee oriented and (b) production oriented.
- The leadership Grid in which managerial/leadership is classified into two styles: (a) concern for result and (b) concern for people.

The behavioral theory advocates leadership styles that emphasize concern for employees, teams, and the organization. The theory promotes a participative style of management and consensus in decision-making. It also encourages leaders to be self-ware of their behavior in organizational settings and to recognize the influence of their behavior on employees' productivity and output. In the context of research findings, scholars have identified several leadership styles including the following:

- People-oriented leadership (e.g., team-orientation, rewarding success).
- Dictatorial leadership (e.g., strict deadlines, unreceptive to other views).
- Opportunistic leadership (e.g., emphasis on performance,

judgement inconsistency).
- Task-oriented leadership e.g., data-orientation, concern for outcomes).
- Status quo leadership (e.g., adherence to company policies, regular reporting).
- Participative leadership (e.g., delegation of authority, openness for feedback)
- Country club leadership (e.g., strong employee-orientation, open to feedback).

Transactional Leadership

The transactional theory of leadership is an approach to managing human resources of the organization. The theory, sometimes referred to as "managerial leadership," views the relationship in the workplace between the leader and employees largely in the context of cost/benefit as is the case in economic transactions in the marketplace.

Employees receive benefits in the form of monetary and nonmonetary incentives for their good performance, while they incur the cost of unacceptable work performance in the form of punishment or reprimand. Key elements of the theory include the following (e.g., Ismail et al, 2010; Odumeru and Ogbonna, I2013; Basar, et al 2021; Skopak and Hadzaihetovie, 2022):

- Results-oriented organizational elements such as structure, procedures, and systems.
- Leaders focus on both positive (rewards) and negative (punishment) reinforcement to get the work properly accomplished.
- Tasks, polices, goals, and chain of command are well-defined.
- Subordinates are instructed, trained, and monitored.
- More emphasis on deadlines, discipline, and performance while less emphasis is placed on employees' creativity, initiatives, or innovation.
- Employees are allowed certain degree of autonomy to perform their assigned tasks.

Transformational Leadership

Transformational leadership has been the most highlighted, researched, and recommended leadership style in recent years. It is about organizational change and development. The transformational leader (e.g., the CEO) is called a change agent. Scholars and researchers have attempted to identify leaders' styles of management to compare with the demand of a dynamic and competitive global environment as well the expectation of shareholders and employees' aspiration. The transformational leadership style is believed to be a unique approach to motivate employees for greater commitment to the organization.

Transformational leadership is defined "as the style of leadership that heightens consciousness of collective interest among the organization's members and helps them to achieve their collective goals" (García-Morales et al, p.1040). Research findings indicate that transformational leadership is a managerial style highly suitable to forward-looking, growth-oriented business firms, as the leader's vision, behavior, and attitude stimulate employees' efforts toward innovation and organizational performance. Research also shows that this type of leadership can benefit both employees and the organization because it seeks to forge a mutual relationship in which the leader and subordinates motivate each other to reach higher levels of organizational performance along with employee satisfaction.

Moreover, transformational leaders bring about human and economic transformation; they generate vision, missions, goals, winning strategies, and a culture of excellence (Givens, p.6). It can be said that the theory represents a model of optimal cooperation between leaders and subordinates. The leaders are believed to be models of integrity and equality in society. Authors have pointed out (Bonsu, Konorti, 2008; Long et al, 2014; Bonsu ,2018; Farahnak et al, 2020) that transformational leaders are described to be:

- Charismatic.
- Effective communicators who can provide a clear sense of purpose and direction.
- Good mentors, coaches, and inspiring.
- Have positive influence on individuals' and teams.

- Able to identify the need for change and motivate subordinates to participate in strategy implementation and organizational transformation.

To sum up this important leadership style, the transformational theory is about:

- Strengthening employees' attitudes, loyalty, and commitment toward the organization.
- Elevating employees' job performance.
- Encouraging employees' creativity and work quality.
- Assisting the organization achieve its strategic goals of excellence and competitiveness.
- Initiating effective organizational change and monitoring progress.

Entrepreneurial Leadership

Entrepreneurial leadership is a leadership theory that emerged from the fields of entrepreneurship and leadership and can be viewed as a distinctive type of managerial leadership style suitable primarily for entrepreneurial business firms. It is defined as a "style of leadership in which the leader emphasizes the group's performance in achieving organizational goals, which includes discovering and exploiting entrepreneurial opportunities" (Davar et al (2021).

The theory has been developed, refined, and presented as an effective approach to managing business firms in a complex and challenging environment. The theory has attracted the attention of researchers and the business community for its novel approach to leadership. Ian C MacMillan and Rita G. McGrath have coined the term entrepreneurial leadership in 2000 in their book titled "The Entrepreneurial Mindset." The authors believe two factors have made it imperative for organizations to adopt entrepreneurial leadership. They are: (i) elevation of environmental uncertainty surrounding the business enterprise in recent years, and (ii) the increasing intensity of domestic and global market competition.

Entrepreneurial Leadership Dimensions

To become an effective leader, the entrepreneur needs to possess at least two distinct sets of personality and organizational competencies such as being a visionary, charismatic, innovator, team organizer, and opportunity finder and exploiter. Scholars have come up with several suggestions concerning the dimensions of entrepreneurial leadership. For instance, it is suggested that entrepreneurial leadership mindset involves three distinct dimensions: (i) people-orientation, (ii) purpose-orientation, and (iii) learning-orientation (e.g., Kassai, 2021).

Al Mamun et al (2018) suggested the dimensions of responsibility, accountability, analytical thinking, and emotional intelligence. On the other hand, Harrison et al (2018) emphasized four entrepreneurial leadership dimensions: technical/business skills, interpersonal skills, conceptual skills, and entrepreneurial skills. Finally, (Davar et al, 2021) introduced a model of entrepreneurial leadership dimensions that include the following:

- Guidance (goal orientation, inspiration, and role modeling).
- Facilitation (perceptual ability, communication ability, and empowerment).
- Supporting (developing commitment, motivation, and emotional intelligence).
- Coaching (team-orientation and participation).
- Entrepreneurship factors (professionalism and entrepreneurial talent).

Chapter Summary

Scholars and researchers have introduced, debated, and refined several leadership theories of which five are discussed in this chapter. The great man (or woman) theory stipulates that some individuals – whether born to powerful families or having unique experiences – can emerge as leaders. Trait theory emphasizes that leaders possess certain personality characteristics that distinguish them from non-leaders.

The behavioral theory of leadership focusses its attention on the behavior of leaders rather than their personality attributes, and that leadership behavior can be taught and learned. The transactional theory of leadership indicates that leaders offer followers incentives to motivate them to exert higher levels of efforts and commitment to the organization.

The transformational theory of leadership is about sharing the vision with employees and improving relationship with them. It is also concerned with connecting employees to the organization's strategic goals and facilitate their learning and empowerment.

The increasing pressure of stockholders and creditors on publicly owned business firms to enhance their performance has induced scholars to introduce the theory of entrepreneurial leadership as an effective leadership style, while, at the same time, urging business leaders to strengthen their managerial skills with entrepreneurial competency and drive.

Research findings indicate that as is the case with transformational leadership, entrepreneurial leadership is an influential motivational style of management for attaining and sustaining creativity, innovation, and productivity in the organization. In conclusion, despite the enormous advantages especially of entrepreneurial leadership style, it seems that no single leadership theory is the "best" approach for all organizations, in all industries, an under all circumstances. As Salazar (1991, p. 130) pointed out that "In some cases, elements of different theories and even the theories themselves can be combined to get the best results."

Chapter Questions

1. What is leadership?
2. How can one become an effective leader?
3. In your judgement, what is the "best" leadership theory? Explain.
4. Discuss the meaning and attributes of entrepreneurial leadership.
5. How can one become an influential entrepreneurial leader? Discuss.

Chapter 16

Team Building for Creativity and Innovation in Organizations

"Great things in business are never done by one person.
They're done by a team of people."

Learning Objectives:

- Appreciate the importance of teams to organizations.
- Review the meaning of teams and the differences between teams and groups.
- Understand the theories of team building.
- Explore the criteria for effective team performance.

Nations are built on teamwork via the creation of small and large projects. The range of projects extends to include such entities as houses, railroads, dams, factories, airplanes, schools, missiles, and so on. Projects, regardless of size or purpose, are essential for a nations' progress and sustainability.

Projects are in turn propelled by individuals experienced in such fields as project management, process engineering, economics, life sciences, and Information Technology (IT) depending on the nature of projects and the industries. In this chapter we address team formation and performance as well as the criteria for individual inclusion in a team.

Teams versus Groups

Are the terms "teams" and "groups" synonymous and, therefore, possess the same attributes or are they different? A team is understood as an assembly of appointed individuals that normally consists of three to nine people and who are expected to provide recommendations or make decisions about certain issues that facilitate the accomplishment of organizational goals.

A group, on the other hand, is defined by the Oxford Languages dictionary as "a number of people or things that are located close together or are considered classed together." Experts provide the main distinctions between teams and groups:

- A team consists of selected individuals to perform some specific tasks while a group is a collection of people or objects for unknown purpose.
- A team is selected for its members' skills or experiences while a group of people is an arbitrary gathering of individuals with unknown skills, talents, or intention.
- A team is driven by organizational necessity for success and growth while a group has no shared organizational goals or purpose.

Teams in Organizations

Organizations are destined to build work teams to achieve their goals and strategies. Teams differ in size and purpose and can be formal or informal. The main team categories are classified as follows: (i) leadership teams that include the CEO, vice presidents of finance, marketing, operations, and so on, (ii) technical teams that include engineers, technicians, designers, and the like, (iii) managerial teams that include departmental managers and supervisors, (iv) ad hoc teams that are created for specific purpose for example, to assess the viability of a business plan or an office building design, (v) cross-functional teams that include expertise form different departments or units in the organization, (vi) self-managed team and (vi) virtual teams.

The last two categories of teams are likely to consist of individuals with a variety of expertise, organizations, and nationalities. In recent years, because of COVID-19 and related health concerns, many teams schedule at least some of the meetings to take place remotely online.

Importance of Teams

The benefits of teams are numerous to organizations. These include teams:

- Help discover individual team members' talents and hone further their competencies.
- Offer a sense of belonging and make the work environment enjoyable.
- Increase work efficiency, quality, and the achievement of company goals.
- Enable team members to learn about products or services and company policies and goals.
- Strengthen team members' critical thinking and creativity.
- Encourage team members to develop leadership attributes.
- Improve the members' technical and communication skills.
- Improve work ethics and organizational commitment.
- Promote understanding among team members of different backgrounds and education.

Characteristics of Effective Teams

A team's effectiveness is measured by the outcomes of its recommendations or decisions which are expected to contribute to the organization's strategic goals such as growth, profitability, and competitive advantage. Team effectiveness, however, depends on a host of interrelated and intertwined factors that include the following:

- The existence of a well-defined problem or issue.
- Clarity of goals and clarity of the roadmap for achieving these goals.
- Team leadership to ensure trust, communication, critical thinking, and divergent opinions.

- Qualifications of team members and their expertise in solving problems or addressing issues.
- Availability of adequate resources as well as top management support.

Attributes of Team Members

Tram members need to possess certain skills and behaviors to be able to contribute to the team's effectiveness and success. These include:

- The ability to communicate ideas in a clear and convincing manner.
- Being open-minded to appreciate different views or unfamiliar ideas and a willingness to discuss them calmly and intellectually.
- Active listening and participation in constructive criticism.
- Motivation to commit and contribute to the accomplishment of the team's goals.
- Becoming familiar with the subject matter at hand as well as industry/sector knowledge.
- Creative thinking and problem-solving.
- Promoting trust and honesty within the team environment.

Team Models

Scholars have attempted to explain the nature of teams in organizations and describe their necessity, structures, functions in addition to offering criteria to assess teams' performance and effectiveness. Scholarly contributions in this field are reflected in the so-called "team models" or "theories" which are the subject of discussion in this section.

Tuckman's Theory

Professor Bruce Tuckman's 1965 "stages of group development" theory is the most influential theoretical contributions in the field of teams and team dynamics. The theory identifies four stages that teams go through: forming, storming, norming, and performing. Adjourning is the fifth stage that was later added. The five stages reflect the lifecycle of a team for a specific project or other assignment, as discussed below:

- **Forming**. This is the introduction stage for the team during which: (i) team members introduce themselves, indicate their formal positions in the organizations and expertise, (ii) the goals of the assignment are discussed as well as its timeline, (iii) resources available to the team are discussed, and (iv) ongoing status meetings are planned.
- **Storming.** It is expected in this stage that: (i) the team becomes more aware of its purpose, (ii) a few team members vie for dominance, (iii) team disagreements and hostility occur, and (iv) the team leader attempts to sort out issues of confusion and disagreement.
- **Norming.** In this stage: (i) the team leader plays a pivotal role to help the team reach agreement on key issues, and (ii) the team tends to demonstrate unity, harmony, and commitment.
- **Preforming.** This stage is characterized by: (i) team autonomy, solidarity, satisfaction, and engagement, (ii) a clear team vision, and (iii) goals and strategies are in sight for achievement.
- **Adjourning.** This is the last stage of the team's assignment during which the group will disband.

Belbin's Team Role Theory

In 1981, Professor Meredith Belbin introduced the "Team Role Theory" on the personality attributes of team members. Clearly, the role of team members has far-reaching consequences on the team's performance as reflected in the success or failure of the team. The assumption is that an individual's attributes are signified in one of nine roles, or patterns of behavior, acted upon by team members.

The roles that team members play determine the functioning of the team as a whole and its ultimate performance. Professor Belbin also created what is known as "Belbin Team Inventory" that can be administered by individual team members with test feedback offered by company consultants or managers. The nine Belbin team roles are indicated below. They are descriptions of attributes of team members:

- Plant (a creative team member with good problem-solving skills).
- Resource Investigator (a member with sound communication skills).
- Coordinator (a member who can define goals and who may be suitable for team leadership).
- Shaper (an energetic and driven member who seeks goal accomplishment).
- Monitor-Evaluator (a member who possesses strategic thinking and good judgement).
- Team Worker (a member who is ready to listen, cooperate, and avoid team conflicts).
- Implementer (a member who is trustworthy and productive).
- Completer (a punctual, perfectionist team member).
- Specialist (a member who reviews issues methodically and thoughtfully).

The GRPI Model

GRPI is a popular model introduced by Professor Richard Beckhard in 1972 to assist business firms in their efforts to build effective work teams. The model is straightforward to learn and adopt because of its simplicity and usefulness. The premise of the model is that: (i) teams are indispensable to organizations, (ii) teams need to be effective to justify their existence, and (iii) team effectiveness is achieved via its development as well as cooperation among its members. The abbreviation "GRPI" stands for Goals, Roles, Processes, and Interpersonal relationships, as explained below:

- Goals (clearly identifiable targets for the team to accomplish).
- Roles (tasks, responsibilities, and authorities of team members need to be clarified as well as the meetings procedures and methods).
- Processes (team communication and collaboration activities are

defined).

- Interpersonal relationships (interactions of team members within an environment of trust, feedback, and compromise).

The Google Model

Google management sponsored an extensive research project to identify the forces that contribute to team effectiveness in an organizational setting. The research findings identified the following key determinants for team effectiveness:

- Psychological safety (the team environment needs to be free from intimidation or disrespect so that team members feel emotionally safe and willing to take risk in discussions).
- Dependability (ability and commitment of team members to meet their obligations and complete assigned tasks on time).
- Structure and clarity (members are fully aware of the team's objectives and the nature of the task).
- Meaning of work (members are aware of the importance of the task at hand and the significance of their contribution to accomplish it as planned).
- Impact of work (the team's work is invaluable for the organizations and its future).

Chapter Summary

Organizations are team-oriented entities. The term "team" refers to a group of individuals assigned to perform a task or series of tasks in accordance with the organization's major goals and objectives. Teams differ in size, purpose, and effectiveness. Teams provide many benefits to the organization including improved operations and products, and they help members improve skills and leadership attributes.

Scholars have developed models, theories, and approaches to guide organizations in their efforts to build creative teams along with effective team performance. Widely discussed models include Tuckman's theory, The GRPI model, and the Google model. Although the models and theories address the same issues, that is, team effectiveness, they differ in terms of analysis and conclusions.

Chapter Questions

1. What are the differences or similarities between teams and groups?
2. Discuss the importance of teams to organizations.
3. Explain the GRPI model.
4. What are the key ingredients of an effective team?
5. How would you go about leading a strategic planning team?

Chapter 17

Artificial Intelligence and the Emergence of New Market Opportunities

> "Some people call this artificial intelligence,
> but the reality is this technology will enhance us.
> So instead of artificial intelligence. I think we'll augment our intelligence."
>
> Ginni Rometty

Learning Objectives:

- Understand the meaning of Artificial Intelligence (AI).
- Recognize the impact of AI on the economy.
- Identify key applications of AI.
- Familiarize yourself with AI market opportunities.

In an article published by the Brookings Education, Indermit[37] made a bold statement, declaring that "Whoever leads in artificial intelligence in 2030 will rule the world until 2100." This statement highlights the growing importance of AI in the world today, particularly in 2023, as

---

37   Indermit, Gill (January 17, 2020). Whoever Leads in Artificial Intelligence in 2030 will Rule the World. until 2100, Brookings Education, https://www.brookings.edu/research/using-big-data-and-artificial-intelligence-to-accelerate-global-development/.

we witness the emergence of numerous applications developed with the help of powerful tools such as ChatGPT, Bing, ChatSonic/ChatWriter, and Phind.

The emergence of the AI revolution has significant implications for entrepreneurial venture creation, opportunity seizing, and innovation. As such, this chapter aims to explore the nature of AI and its impact on the U.S. economy, industrial progress, supply chain, the introduction of new and improved products, as well as job creation and destruction.

What is AI?

To explore the long-term potential of AI and the window of opportunities AI opens for entrepreneurs, it is important to address questions such as "What is AI?" and "What is AI's impact to society at large?". Additionally, it is important to understand AI related technologies that have played a vital role in the creation of AI. To begin, in late 1980s, computer scientist Schank stated that "Artificial intelligence involves the study of how to make computers do things which, at the moment, people do better. This requires that we figure out what it is that people do when they are solving problems and then try to get computers to do the same kinds of things."[38]

However, in recent years, rapid scientific progress has led to more comprehensive definitions of AI, such as "Artificial intelligence is the application of rapid data processing, machine learning, predictive analysis, and automation to simulate intelligent behavior and problem-solving capabilities with machines and software."[39]. Another definition emphasizes that "It is the science and engineering of making intelligent machines, especially intelligent computer programs. It is related to the similar task of using computers to understand human intelligence, but AI does not have to confine itself to methods that are biologically observable."[40]

---

38   Schank, R. C. (1987). What is AI, Anyhow" *AI Magazine*, 4(8).
39   Deepai.org, https://deepai.org/machine-learning-glossary-and-terms/artificial-intelligence. Retrieved on March 2023.
40   IBM indicated that the above definition was offered by John McCarthy, a computer scientist, https://www.ibm.com/cloud/learn/what-is-artificial-intelligence. Retrieved in March 2023. Retrieved in March 2023.

An examination of supplementary explanations uncovers that AI encompasses a scientific domain that incorporates a range of inputs, such as:

- Powerful computers.
- Complex software development and applications such as deep learning and machine learning.
- Algorithms.
- Specialized human skills and superior expertise.
- Advanced data processing and prediction.
- Natural language.
- Cloud computing.
- Team cooperation.

AI has been developed to assist organizations, societies, and individuals in a variety of activities, including:

- To help solve complex problems and aid in decision-making in areas such as the environment, agriculture, transportation, and the medical field.
- To automate tasks, operations, and other activities.
- To improve efficiency, increase output, and enhance the quality of products.
- To pave the way for the creation of new businesses and industries.
- To support education and learning.
- To assist business firms in their quest for competitive advantage.
- To contribute to national economic and military power.

As AI continues to progress in the coming years, new market opportunities will emerge, new jobs will be created, some jobs will disappear[41], and new wealth will be generated. Therefore, entrepreneurs need to study the AI revolution, understand its implications, and become more innovative in opportunity identification and exploitation.

AI Technologies

It has become apparent in recent years that AI is quickly expanding its domain and sphere of influence especially in economically advanced societies such as the United States. Consequently, several higher education institutions including the University of Pennsylvania, Stanford University, Carnegie Mellon University, Massachusetts Institute of Technology, Oxford University, and the University of Toronto have established advanced programs of research and study in the AI field[42]. Table 1 below shows key AI related technologies that are being developed and utilized in various business firms and industries:

---

41   For example, in examining the possible consequences of large language models (LLMs), such as Generative Pretrained Transformers (GPTs), on the U.S. labor market, a recent study discovered that the implementation of LLMs could affect at least 10 percent of the work tasks for around 80 percent of the U.S. workforce. Additionally, roughly 19 percent of workers could have at least 50 percent of their tasks impacted {Eloundou, Tyna et al (March, 23, 2023). GPTs are GPTs: An Early Look at the Labor Market Impact Potential of Large Language Models, Working Paper, University of Pennsylvania}.

42   The following Website lists 20 Best Artificial Intelligence schools for college students in the United States, https://www.computersciencedegreehub.com/best/artificial-intelligence-engineering-schools/.

Table 1

AI-Related Technologies

Machine learning	Deep learning	Robotics
Neural networks	Computer vision	Genetic algorithms
Natural Language Processing (NLP)	Expert systems	Decision trees
Fuzzy logic	Evolutionary algorithms	Pattern recognition
Artificial neural networks	Swarm intelligence	Augmented Reality (AR)
Image recognition	Virtual reality (VR)	Speech recognition
Predictive analytics	Data mining	Big data
Cloud computing	Internet of Things (IoT)	Autonomous vehicles
Chatbots	Machine vision	Cognitive computing
Quantum computing	Blockchain technology	Cybersecurity
Speech recognition	Virtual agents	Peer to Peer Networks
Generative AI	Digital twins	Knowledge Worker Aid

Sources: See. For example, Pedamkar, Priya. Artificial Intelligence Technology, https://www.educba.com/artificial-intelligence-technology; Daley, Sam. 36 Artificial Intelligence Examples Shaking Up Business Across Industries, https://builtin.com/artificial-intelligence/examples-ai-in-industry. Marr, Bernard. The 5 Biggest Artificial Intelligence (AI) Trends In 2023, https://www.forbes.com/sites/bernardmarr/2022/10/10/the-5-biggest-artificial-intelligence-ai-trends-in-2023/?sh=5dfa34c21d3d.

AI is a powerful tool that is essential in increasing the probability of business success and effectiveness. Recent reports indicate that many firms have been embracing various forms of AI-related technologies. For instance, Gurtu[43] asserted that AI has been adopted in a variety of industries including healthcare, automotive, finance, transportation, and E-commerce.

---

43   Gurtu, Anurag (January 2021). Five Industries Reaping The Benefits Of Artificial Intelligence, Forbes, Five Industries Reaping The Benefits Of Artificial Intelligence (forbes.com). Retrieved on March 2023.

AI Business Opportunities

The US and other countries[44] are progressively shifting towards an AI-driven economy where nearly all products and business activities will be powered by this technology and its related branches. The new economy is expected to be dominated by innovative entrepreneurial ventures and business firms. As of early 2023, AI is revolutionizing business opportunities in various industries as well as the field of entrepreneurship.

One application of AI within the field of finance, for instance, is the use of robo-advisers that create personalized investment portfolios. Additionally, AI is becoming the leading technology in detecting fraud by identifying transaction abnormalities and inconsistencies that require management investigation to prevent significant financial harm to businesses.

In the realm of Big Data, AI allows business owners to leverage vast amounts of information to make data-driven decisions that can accelerate business growth. AI-powered tools have applications in various organizational functions and activities, such as writing assistants that can produce high-quality articles and essays in a remarkably short time. These assistants and productivity tools can be utilized in areas like copywriting, marketing, and beyond.

AI Language Models

In early 2023, several innovative technologies have appeared on the market such as OpenAI GPT-4 and Microsoft Bing. These

---

44   Reports from Vanguard Advisors indicate that the global economy, as estimated by the International Monetary System, reached $104 trillion in 2022 (http://www.advisors.vanguard.com). Meanwhile, the U.S. Bureau of Economic Analysis reported that the United States economy was estimated at $24.46 trillion, which represents approximately 24 percent of the global economy for the same year (https://www.bea.gov). These figures are worth noting to visualize the magnitude of entrepreneurial opportunities in the country and elsewhere around the world.

productivity, high-performance tools, that are growing in popularity and applications, have opened lucrative windows of opportunity for entrepreneurs and other business-minded individuals.

AI language models are trained to be capable of writing and speaking in ways that appear as they were real humans with amazing common sense. They are even designed to make jokes and entertain those of us who contact them. AI language models are capable of performing a variety of functions. In an informative article, Cem Dilmegani, reviewed 70 generative AI applications as shown in Table 2 below[45]:

Table 2

Selected Generative AI Applications

Image generation	3D Shape Generation	Music Generation	Audience research
Semantic Image-to-Photo Translation	Text Generation	Code generation	Code completion
Image-to-Image Conversion	Sentiment analysis	Bug fixing	Conversational AI
Image Resolution Increase	Data Synthesis	Video Prediction	Tutoring
Streamlined drug discovery	Personalized medicine	Course design	Generating video ads
Speech-to-Speech Conversion	Personalized lessons	Player behavior analysis	Game testing
Creative fashion designing	Turning sketches into color image	Customer Service	Creating customer emails
Text-to-Speech Generator	Marketing & Trend Analysis	Answering FAQs	Content creation for Marketing
Personalized content creation	Risk management	Generating topic idea	Grouping search intent
Population health management	Data privacy protection	Creating sitemap codes	Creating interview questions
Sales forecasting	Lead identification	Contract compliance	Contract generation

Source: Dilmegani, Cem. 70+ Generative AI Applications/Use Cases in 2023, *AI Multiple*.https://research.aimultiple.com/generative-ai-applications.

Skills Gap

45   Dilmegani, Cem. 70+ Generative AI Applications/Use Cases in 2023, AI Multiple.

The U.S. economy is growing and is showing resilience and resourcefulness. According to data, the demand for skilled workers is also growing at a rate that outstrips the country's population growth rate. For instance, in late July 2021, the Bureau of Labor Statistics reported that there were 10.9 million job openings, indicating a significant employment opportunity for individuals with the necessary skills. However, the economy faces the obstacle of a relative scarcity of highly qualified workers to meet the increasing demand of AI and related technologies. Many industries demonstrate the existence of a skills gap.

The country can achieve its national and global strategic goals through skillful workforce, innovation, investment, and entrepreneurship. National employment is essential for income, output, and economic growth. It also drives education, innovation, and competitive advantage. The magnitude of employment and its sector distribution depends on various factors, including consumer demand, private investment, government expenditures, workforce skills, and productivity.

The county is destined for a new economy in the foreseeable future. For example, Fuei[46] stated that the digitization of the economy is likely to change the types of future occupations in societies. Aghion[47] pointed out that non-educated employees will be more negatively affected in the future by robotization than educated individuals. Binder and Bound[48] discussed the declining job opportunities for individuals with fewer skills and less education. Moreover, Fey and Osborne[49] of Oxford University estimated that about 47 percent of U.S. total employment is at risk of computerization (i.e., automation).

The national goals of technological advancement, competitive advantage, and rapid economic growth make it imperative for the U.S.

46   Fuei, King L. (2017). Automation, Computerization and Future Employment in Singapore, *Journal of Southeast Asian Economies*, 34(2), 388-399.
47   Aghion, Philippe et al (2019). Artificial Intelligence, Growth and Employment: The Role of Policy, Economie & Statistique, Issue 510-511-512, 149-164.
48   Binder, Ariel J. and Bound, John (2019). The Declining Labor Market Prospects of Less-Educated Men, *Journal of Economic Perspectives*, 33(2), 163-190.
49   Frey, Carl Benedikt and Osborn, Michael (2013). The Future of Employment: How susceptible are jobs to Computerisation? Working Paper, Oxford Martin School, Oxford University

workforce to be skillful, productive, and competitive. While some skills are deemed essential for all occupations and sectors of the economy (e.g., effective communication), other skills (e.g., stock analysis) are industry- or company-specific. Career Guide Indeed[50] has identified the following skills as being in high demand in today's job market:

- Artificial intelligence
- Cloud computing
- Blockchain and software development
- Industrial design
- Animation and video production
- Creativity and analysis
- Collaboration, adaptability, and team management.

Entrepreneurship demands a diverse set of human abilities to fulfill the needs of the evolving economy. These abilities include technical expertise, strategic thinking, financial acumen, industry, and market comprehension. However, a shortage of these skills can impede the short-term growth of entrepreneurial ventures and hinder the overall economic advancement of a country.

Despite these challenges, entrepreneurs can play a crucial role in mitigating the skills gap, along with the assistance of educational institutions and government agencies. To elaborate, academic institutions can enhance their specialized graduate and undergraduate programs in entrepreneurship-related fields. Additionally, governmental entities such as the U.S. Small Business Administration and state-level economic development agencies can provide entrepreneurship training programs to bridge the skills gap.

Chapter Summary

AI is rapidly becoming an essential tool for entrepreneurs and businesses, revolutionizing the way business operations are conducted. Its widespread applications in finance, industrial production, the

---

50   Indeed, Career Guide, https://www.indeed.com/career-advice/finding-a-job/in-demand-skills

medical field, and supply chain are well-documented. As a revolutionary technology, AI is expected to transform economies as it increasingly becomes an integral part of daily life for both national and global populations.

While it is likely that AI will lead to the disappearance of millions of jobs in the coming years, it will also help create millions of others. For instance, a recent study[51] examining the possible consequences of large language models (LLMs), such as Generative Pretrained Transformers (GPTs), on the U.S. labor market suggests that LLMs' implementation could impact at least 10 percent of work tasks for around 80 percent of the U.S. workforce.

Moreover, roughly 19 percent of workers could see at least 50 percent of their tasks affected. Despite these potential job losses, AI will also enable entrepreneurs to establish innovative and sustainable businesses in numerous fields, including transportation, software development, robotics, communication, consumer products and services, and other ventures.

Chapter Questions

1. Explain the meaning of AI.
2. Elaborate on some of the AI-related technologies.
3. Discuss the impact of AI on job creation and destruction.
4. What is in your judgement the future of AI?
5. How would you go about deploying AI technologies in your venture?

---

51   Eloundou, Tyna et al (March, 23, 2023). GPTs are GPTs: An Early Look at the Labor Market Impact Potential of Large Language Models, Working Paper, University of Pennsylvania.

References

Abd Aziz, Zarith D. et al (2022). The Influence of Entrepreneurial Ecosystem on SMEs Industry
in Malaysia, *Advances in Social Sciences Research Journal*, 9(10), 348-356.

Abdelgawad, Sondos and Zahra, Shaker A. (2020). Family Firms' Religious Identity and
Strategic Renewal, *Journal of Business Ethics*, 163(4), 775-787.

Abouzeedan, Adli and Hedner, Thomas (2012). Organization structure theories and open
innovation paradigm, World Journal of Science, Technology, and Sustainable Development, 9(1), 6-27.

Abrams, Rhonda (2012). *Entrepreneurship*, Palo Alto: California, Planningshop.

Aghion, Philippe et al (2019). Artificial Intelligence, Growth and Employment: The Role of
Policy, Economie & Statistique, Issue 510-511-512, 149-164.

Agrawal, Ajay et al (2017). What to Expect from Artificial Intelligence, *MIT Sloan*
Management? Review, 58(3), 22-26.

Ahiaga-Dagbui, Dominic D. et al (2020). Building high-performing and integrated project teams,
Engineering, Construction, and Architectural Management, 27(10), 334103361.

Al-Dajani, Haya et al (2014). Gender and Family Business: New Theoretical Directions,
*International Journal of Gender and Entrepreneurshi*p, 6(3).

Aloulou, Wassim (2018). Examining Entrepreneurial Orientation's Dimensions – Performance

Relationship in Saudi Family Businesses: Contingency Role of Family Involvement in Management, *Journal of Family Business*, 8(2), 126-143.

Alsaaty, Falih M. and Makhlouf, Hany H. (2007). *Entrepreneurship: Launching and Managing*
New Ventures. Maryland: Publish America.

Alsaaty, Falih M. and Makhlouf, Hany H. (2012). *The Entrepreneurial Reach*, Pennsylvania:
World Association Publishers.

Alaslani, Mohammad and Collins, Jock (2017). The Blocked Mobility Hypothesis and Muslim
Immigrant Entrepreneurship in Sydney, Australia, *Revie of Integrative Business and*
Economics Research, 6(3), 333-357.

Alsever, Jennifer (2009). How to Innovate: A step-by-step guide to Fostering Business
Creativity, FBS: Fortune Small Business, vol. 19, no. 8, pp. 68-75.

Altshuller, G. S. (1984). *Creativity as an Exact Science*, translated by Anthony Williams, New
York: Gordon and Breach Science Publishers

Ardichvili, Alexander, Cardozo Richard, and Sourav, Ray (2003). A Theory of Entrepreneurial   Opportunity   Identification   and Development, *Journal of Business Venturing*, vol. 18.
No. 1,105-123.

Astrachan, Joseph H. and Shanker, Melissa C. (2003). Family Businesses' Contribution to
the U.S. Economy: A Closer Look, *Family Business Review*, 16(3), 211-219.

Awotoye, Yemisi F. and Sing, Robert P. (2018). Immigrant entrepreneurs in the USA: A
Conceptual Discussion of the Demands of Immigration and Entrepreneurial Intentions, *New England Journal of Entrepreneurship*, 21(2), 123-139.

Azoulay, Pierre et al (2020). Immigration and Entrepreneurship in the United States, *Working*
Paper Series 27778, National Bureau of Economic Research.

Bair, Stephanie P. (2022). Innovation's Hidden Externalities, Brigham Young University Law
Review, 47(5), 1385-1433.

Barba-sánchez, Virginia and Atienza-sahuquillo, Carlos (2017). Entrepreneurial Motivation
and Self-employment: Evidence from Expectancy Theory, *International Entrepreneurship and Management Journal*, 13(4), 1097-1115.

Baron, Robert (2006). Opportunity Recognition as Pattern Recognition: How Entrepreneurs
'Connect the Dots' to Identify New Business Opportunities, *Academy of Management Perspectives* 227(12), 104-119.

Baron, Robert (2004). Opportunity Recognition: A Cognitive Perspective, *Academy of*
Management Beat Conference Paper A1-A6.

Barry, Katie, Domb, Ellen, and Slocum, Michael. *TRIZ – What Is TRIZ.* The TRIZ Journal.

Basar, Ufuk et al (2021). A Conceptual Study on the Theoretical Framework of Transformational
and Transactional Leadership Models, *Business & Management Studies*, 9(4), 1708-1720.

Beehr, Terry A. et al (1997). Working in Small Family Businesses: Empirical.

Bernstein, Shai et al (2018). The Contribution of High-Skilled Immigrants to Innovation in the
United States, *Working Papers,* No. 3748, Sandford Graduate School of Business.

Binder, Ariel J. and Bound, John (2019). The Declining Labor Market Prospects of Less-
Educated Men, *Journal of Economic Perspectives*, 33(2), 163-190.

Bingham, Christopher B. and McDonald, Rory M. (2022). Mastering Innovation's Toughest
Trade-Offs, *MIT Sloan Management Review*, 63(4), 66-72.

Bonsu, Samuel (2018). Leadership Style in the Global Economy: A Focus on Cross-Cultural and
Transformational Leadership, *Journal of Marketing and*

Management, 9(2), 37-52.

Brieger, Steven A. and Gielnik, Michael M. (2021). Understanding the Gender Gap in

Immigrant Entrepreneurship: a Multi-country Study of Immigrants' Embeddedness in Economic, Social, and Institutional Contexts, *Small Business Economics*, 56(3), 1007-1031.

Brink, Tove (2014). The Impact on Growth of Outside-In and Inside-Out Innovation in SME

Network Contexts, *International Journal of Innovation Management*, 18(4), 1-11.

Brundin, Ethel et al (2014). Family ownership logic: Framing the core characteristics of family

businesses, *Journal of management and Organization*, 20(1), 6-37.

California State University/Chico, https://www.csuchico.edu/curee/entrepreneur.shtml.

Cappelli, Peter (2015). Skill Gaps, Skill Shortages, and Skill Mismatches: Evidence and

Arguments for the United States, *Industrial & Labor Relations Review*, 68(2), 251.

Caruso, Shirley, J. (2021). Organizational Development: Definition, Uses, and Techniques,

HRdevelopmentinfo, https://harddevelopment.com.

Certo, Samuel C. and Certo, Trevis S (2014). *Modern Management – Concepts and*

Skills, Boston: Pearson Education, Inc.

Chakravorty, N. N. T.(2019). How Does Immigration Impact Output, Employment and Wages?

Evidence from United Kingdom, 19(5), 26-54.

Chami, Ralph (2001). What is Different About Family Businesses? *IMF Working Paper*,

Chandler, G.N. et al (2005). Antecedents and Exploitation Outcomes of Opportunity

Identification Process. *Academy of Management* Best Conference paper, J1-J6.

Chelly, Amine (2011). Searching for Opportunities and Opportunity

Discovery: An Extension of
>Bhave's (1994) Work, *ICSB World Conference Proceedings*, Council for Small Business.

Cherukara, Joseph M. and Manalel, James (2011). Evolution of Entrepreneurship Theories
>through Different Schools of Thought, *the Ninth Biennial Conference on*
>*Entrepreneurship at EDI, Ahmedabad.*

Chirapanda, Suthawan (2020). Identification of Success Factors for Sustainability in
>Family Businesses: Case Study Method and Exploratory Research in Japan, Journal of Family Business Management, 10)1), 58-54.

Christensen, Clayton M. (1977). *The Innovator's Dilemma*, New York, HarperBusiness, Inc.

Christensen, Clayton M; Johnson, Mark W; Rigby, Darrell K. (2002). Foundation of Growth,
>*MIT Sloan Management Review*, 43(3), 22-31.

Christensen, Clayton M. and Raynor, Michael E (2003). *The Innovator's Solution*, Harvard
>Business School Publishing Corporation.

Christensen, Clayton, M. (2006). The Innovator's Dilemma, New York: Collins Business
>Essentials.

Christensen, Clayton M.; Raynor, Michael; McDonald, Rory (2015). What Is Disruptive
>Innovation? *Harvard Business Review*, 93 (12), 44-53.

Claudia, Binz A. and Botero, Isabel C. (2018). We are a Family Firm": An Exploration of the
>Motives for Communicating the Family Business Brand, *Journal of Family Business Management*, 8(1), 2-21.

Conway Center for Family Business, Family Business Facts, www. familybusiness center.com.

Craig, Justin B. et al (2008). Leveraging Family-Based Brand Identity to Enhance Firm
>Competitiveness and Performance in Family Businesses, *Journal of Small Business*

Management, 46(3), 351-371.

Croteau, Martin and Grant, Kenneth (2021). Estimating the Scale of Angel Investment Activity

in Canada: A Comparative Analysis, *Journal of Applied Business and Economics*, 23(2), 170-183.

Davar, Taghi et al (2021). Presenting the Entrepreneurial Leadership Model Based on the

Quantitative Approach of Grounded theory, Quarterly *Public Organizations*

Management, 9(2), 105-120.

David, Fred R. and David, Forest R. (2020). *Strategic Management*, New Jersey:

Pearson/ Prentice- Hall, Inc.

Della-Giustina, Janet L. et al (2022). Quality of Work life Program through Employee

Motivation, *Professional Safety*, 67(10), 3-27.

Delmar, Frederic and Scott, Shane (2003). Does Business Planning Facilitate the development of

New Ventures? *Strategic Management Journal*, 24(12), 1165

Dess, Gregory G; Lumpkin, G. T; Eisner, Alan B. (2008). *Strategic Management,* New York:

McGraw-Hill/Irwin, Inc.

DeTienne, Dawn T. and Chandler, G.N. (2004). Opportunity Identification and its Role in the   Entrepreneurial Classroom: A Pedagogical Approach and Empirical Test, Academy of

Management Learning & Education, vol. 3, no. 3, 242-267.

DiGirolamo, Joel (2010). The art, psychology, and science of management—an

integrated approach. Leaders and the Leadership Process, Turbocharged

Leadership.

Digitalsilk.com, https://www.digitalsilk.com/business-life-cycle-stages

Drucker, Peter F (1954). The Practice of Management, New York: Harper & Row,

Publishers, Inc.

Drucker, Peter F (2001). The Essential Drucker, New York,

HarperCollins Publishers.

Druqus, Liviu (2010). On Management: Is it Scientific Management? No! Is it
Management Science? No! Is it Changing Management? YES!, *Economy Transdisciplinarity Cognition*, 13(1), 5A-6A}.

Duhigg, Charles (Feb. 25, 2016). *What Google Learned From Its Quest to Build the Perfect Team*. New York Times

Family Business, (September/October 2015), The World's Oldest Family Companies,
www.griequity.com.

Fapohunda, Tinuke M. (2013). Towards Effective Team Building in the Workplace,
International Journal of Education and Research, 1(4), 1-12.

Farahnak, Lauren R. et al (2020). The Influence of Transformational Leadership and Leader
Attitudes on Subordinate Attitudes and Implementation Success, *Journal of Leadership & Organizational Studies,* 27(1), 98–111.

Fisher, Monica and Lewin, Paul A. (2018). Push and Pull Factors and Hispanic Helf-
employment in the USA, *Small Business Economics*, 51(4), 1055-1070

Fisher, S.G. et al (2000). The Distribution of Belbin Team Roles among UK Managers,
Personnel Review, 29(2), 124-140.

Forbes (July 17, 2011). In Pictures: 15 Oldest Family Companies,
https://www.forbes.com/2011/06/17/oldest-family-businesses_slide.html.

Fröhlich, Donckels, E. (1991). Are Family Businesses Really Different? European Experiences
from STATOS, Wiley Online Library, https://onlinelibrary.wiley.com/doi/10.1111/j.1741-6248.1991.00149.x.

Fuller, Mark (2022). Wheat and Chaff: The Degree to which Strategic Management Principles
are Integrated within Corporate Social Responsibility

Reporting among Large Canadian Firms, *International Journal of Corporate Social Responsibilities*, 7(1).

García-Morales, Victor J. et al (2011). Transformational leadership influence on organizational
performance through organizational learning and innovation, *Journal of Business Research*, 65, 1040-1050.

Ghatak, Sanchita and Sing, Surabhi (2019). Examining Maslow's Hierarchy Need Theory in the
Social Media Adoption, *FIIB Business Review*, 8(4), 292-302.

Ghazzi, Antonio (2013). Revisiting Business Strategy under Discontinuity, *Management
Decision*, 51(7), 1326.

Gioia, Dennis A. and Pure, Evelyn (1990), Multiparadigm Perspectives on Theory Building,
Academy of Management Review, 15(4), 584-602.

Gomes, Sofia and Ferreira, Pedro (2022). Entrepreneurial activity and economic growth: A
dynamic data panel analysis of European countries, *Entrepreneurial Business and Economics Review*, 10(2), 7-20.

Gurchiek, Kathy (2009). Motivating Innovation, HR Magazine, vol. 54, no. 9, pp. 30-35.

Habberston, Timothy G. and Williams Mary L. (1999). A Resource-Based Framework for
Assessing the Strategic Advantages of Family Firms, *Family Business Review*, 12(1), 1-25.

Hansson, Per (2015). Resource Based Theory and Family Business in *Theoretical Perspectives*
on *Family businesses*, Matthias, Nordqvist et al (editors), Edward Elgar Publishing,
http://www.diva-portal.org/smash/record.jsf?pid=diva2%3A1054946&dswid=-1699

Haque, MD; Liu Li; Amayah, Angela T(2020). The Relationship Between Vision and
Organizational Readiness for Change: The Mediating

Effects of Empowerment and Trust in the Leader, *Journal of Organizational Psychology*, 20(2),159-174.

Harrison, Christian et al (2018). Entrepreneurial Leadership in a Developing economy: A Skill-
based Analysis, *Journal of Small Business and Enterprise Development*, 24(3), 521-548.

Hatten, Timothy S. (2020). *Small Business Management*, Los Angeles: California, Sage
Publications, Inc.

Head, Thomas, C. (2011). Douglas McGregor's legacy: lessons learned, lessons lost, Journal of
Management History, 17(2), 202-216.

Heidi, Neck M. et al (2018). *Entrepreneurship*, Sage Publishing, Los Angeles: California.

Hill, Charles W. and Jones, Gareth, R. (2013). *Strategic Management Theory*, Mason: Ohio,
South-Western, Inc.

Hill, Charles W et al (2020). *Strategic Management*, Boston: MA, Cengage Learning, Inc.

Hisrich, Robert D. and Peters, Michael P. (2002). *Entrepreneurship*, Boston: Massachusetts,
McGraw-Hill/ Irwin.

Hoffman, James et al (2006). Achieving Sustained Competitive Advantage: A Family Capital
Theory, *family Business Review*, 19(2), 135-145.

Ida, Farida and Setiawan, Doddy (2022). Business Strategies and Competitive Advantage: The
Role of Performance and Innovation, *Journal of Open Innovation: Technology Market*
and Complexity, 8(3), 163.

International Organization for Migration, *World Migration Report, 2020*,
https://publications.iom.int/system/files/pdf/wmr_2020.pdf

Isenberg, D. J. (2011). The entrepreneurship ecosystem strategy as a new paradigm for economic
policy: principles for cultivating entrepreneurship. Presentation at the Institute of

International and European Affairs, Dublin.

Islam, Md Zohurul et al (2022). Practices of Fayol's Principles in Bangladesh Public Sector

Organizations: An Empirical Evidence, *Journal of Management Research*, 22(1), 39-50.

Islam, Shk Imran and Ayupp, Kartinah (2022). Innovation is the Way Forward: The

Impact of Organisational Culture on Innovation in the United Arab Emirates (UAE), *Economic Affairs*, 67(4), 463-470.

Ismail et al (2010). Transformational and Transactional Leaders Styles as a Predictor of

Individual Outcomes, *Theoretical and Applied Economics*, 6(547), 89-104

Jefferson, Marlon M. et al (2020). Family as an Institution: The Influence of Institutional Forces

in Transgenerational Family Businesses, *International Journal of Entrepreneurial Behavior & Research*, 26(1), 54-75.

Jeong, Harry et al (2021). Development of Food Packaging through TRIZ and the Possibility of

Open Innovation, *Journal of Open Innovation*, 7(4), 213.

Jones, Alex (2019). The Tuckerman's Model Implementation, Effect, and Analysis & the New

Development of Jones LSI Model on a Small Group, *Journal of Management, 6(4),*

23-28.

Jones, Gareth R. and George, Jennifer M. (2014). *Contemporary Management*, New York:

McGraw-Hill, Inc.

Kamasak, Rifat et al (2017). Quantitative Methods in Organizational Research: An Example of

Grounded Theory Data Analysis in Christiansen, Bryn and Chandan, Harish C., *Handbook of Research on Organizational Culture and Diversity in the Modern Workforce*, SCOPUS.

Kantabutra, Sooksan and Vimolratana, Pisanu (2009). Vision-based Leadership:

Relationships and Consequences in Thai and Australian

Retail Stores, *Pacific Journal of Business Administration*, 1(2), 165-188.

Karikari, Amoa-Gyarteng and Shephare, Dhiwayo (2022). The Impact of Capital Structure on
Profitability of Nascent Small and Medium Enterprises in Ghana, *Journal of Business and Economic Research*, 17(2), 275-291.

Karimkhani, Mehrdad et al (2022). Identifying and Prioritizing Factors Affecting Innovation of
Investee Companies From the Perspective of Venture Capitalists: A Case Study, 15(3), 633-648.

Kassai, Ákos (2021). The Four Leadership Styles of Entrepreneurs, *Management Review*, 53(5),
16-31.

Kauffaman.org/ecosystem-playbook-draft-3/glossary-and-resources/

Kavas, Mustafa et al (2020). Islamic Family Business: The Constitutive Role of Religion in
Business, *Journal of Business Ethics*, 163(4(, 689-700.

Kemp, Linzi J. (2013). Modern to Postmodern Management: Developments in Scientific
Management, *Journal of Management History*, 19(3), 345-361.

King, Andrew A. and Baljir, Baatartogtokh (2015). How Useful is the Theory of Disruptive In
novation? MIT Sloan Management Journal Review, 57(1), 76-90.

Kjellman, Andrews J. (2014). Family Business Explained by Field Theory, *Journal of Family*
Business Management, 4(2), 194-212.

Konorti, Eli P. (2008). The 3D Transformational Leadership Model, *The Journal of American*
Academy of Business, 14(1), 10-20

Kopelman, Richard E. et al (2008). Douglas McGregor's Theory X and Y: Toward a
Construct-valid Measure, *Journal of Management Issues*, 20(2), 159-160}.

Krichevskiy, Dmitriy et al (2016). Does the Level of Economic Development and the Market
Size of Immigrants' Country of Birth Matter for their Engagement in Entrepreneurial Activities in the USA? Evidence from the Princeton's New Immigrant Surveys of 2003 and 2007, *Journal of Small Business and Entrepreneurship*, 28(3), 223-249.
Kula, Veysel and Tatoglu, Ekrem (2006). Board process attributes and company performance of
family-owned businesses in Turkey, Corporate Governance, 6(5), 624-634.
Leibell, David T. (2010). Family Business McKinsey Report Identifies Five Attributes for
Success, *Trust & Estate*, 149(11), 16.
Leicher, Veronika and Mulder, Reina H. (2016). Team learning, Team Performance and Safe
Team Climate in Elder Care Nursing, *Team Performance Management*, 22(7/8), 399-414
LIanos-Contreras, Orlando A. and Jabri, Muayyad (2019). Exploring Family Business Decline
with Socioemotional Wealth Perspective, *Academia*, 32(1), 63-78.
Liao, Jianwen (Jon) and Gartner William B. (2007/2008). The Influence of Pre-Venture Planning
on New Venture Creation, *Journal of Small Business Strategy,18(2), 1-21.*
Lindsay, Noel J. and Craig, Justin (2002). A Framework for Understanding Opportunities
Recognition: Entrepreneurs Versus Private Equity Financiers. The Journal of Private Equity 6(1), 13-24.
Liu, Weiping et al (2012). Does family business excel in firm performance? An institution-based
view, *Asia Pacific Journal of Management*, 29(4), 965-987.
Long, Choi S. et al (2014). The Impact of Transformational Leadership Style on Job Satisfaction,
World Applied Sciences Journal 29 (1), 117-124
Long, Dan et al (2016). Antecedent factors of business planning in

the new venture emergence in
> China, *Chinese Management Studies*, 10(3), 510-526.

MacMillan, Ian C. and McGrath, Rita G. (2000). *The Entrepreneurial Mindset*, Boston, Harvard
> Business Review Pres, Chapter 12.

Mahmoud M. and Shreteh, Dalal (2021). The Nexus Relationship between Entrepreneurship
> and Economic Growth Dynamic: Evidence from Selected MENA Countries, *International Economic Policy*, 35, 56-75.

Malik, Sikandar H. et al (2014). Leadership Behavior and Acceptance of Leaders by
> Subordinates: Application of Path Goal Theory in Telecom Sector, *International Journal of Trade, Economics and Finance*, 5(2), 170-179.

Martinez-Vergara, Sucet J. and Valls-Pasola, Jaume (2021). Clarifying the disruptive
> innovation puzzle: a critical review, *European Journal of Innovation Management*, 24(3), 893-918

Mathushan, P. and Kengatharan, N. (2022). Human Resources Management Practices and Firm
> Innovation: Mediating Role of Human Capital.

McKee, Annie (2014). *Management*, Boston: MA, Pearson Education, Inc.

Mendonca, Lenny (2009). The 10 Trends You Have to Watch, Harvard Business Review,
> vol. 87, no. 7, pp. 55-60.

Mickan, Sharon and Roger, Sylvia (2000). Characteristics of Effective Teams: a Literature Re
> view, Australian Health Review, 23(3), 201-208.

Minter, Steve (2014). Innovation: Is the U.S. at Risk in the Global Innovation Race? Industry
> week, 263(4), 37-37.

Muhammad, Naveed, L. and Ahmad, Maha (2022). The Entrepreneur's Quest: Qualitative
> Inquiry into the Inspirations and Strategies for Startup in Pakistan, *Pakistan Economic and Social Review*, 58(1), 61-

71.

Murphy, Kyan (2017). Immigration and its Effect on Economic Freedom: Empirical
Approach, *Cato Journal*, 37(3), 531-538).

Mybusiness.com, https://www.mybusiness.com.au/management/ owned.

Neck, Heidi M. et al (2018). *Entrepreneurship*, Los Angeles: California, Sage Publications, Inc.

Nelson, Debra L. and Quick, James C (2006). *Organizational Behavior*, Mason: Ohio, South-
Western, Thompson, Inc.

New York Angels.com (www.newyorkangels.com).

Northouse, Peter G. (2019). *Leadership: Theory and Practice*, Los Angeles, California, Sage
Publishing, Inc.

Odumeru, James A. and Ogbonna, Ifeanyi G. (2013). Transformational vs. Transactional
Leadership Theories: Evidence in Literature, *International Review of Management and Business Research*, 2(2), 355-361.

OECD (2005). Oslo Manual, the Measurement of Scientific and Technological
Innovations.

Omar, Hussam (2011). Arab American Entrepreneurs in San Antonio, Texas: Motivation for
Entry into Self-employment, *Education, Business and Society: Contemporary Middle Eastern Issues*, 4(1), 33-42.

Onorato, Michael and Zhu, Jishan (2019). Building Students' Team Leadership Skills in Higher
Education, *Academy of Business Research Journal*, 2. 54-72.

Organ, Dennis W. (1996). Leadership: The Great Man Theory Revisited, *Business Horizon*,
39(3), 1-4.

Orloff, Michael (2006). *Inventive Thinking through TRIZ*, Berlin: Germany, Modern TRIZ

O'Sullivan, David and Dooly, Lawrence (2009). Applying Innovation, London, Sage

Publication, Inc.

Pandzic, Lejla and Hadziahmetovic, Nereida (2022). The Impact of Intrinsic Rewards on

> Employee Engagement in The Food Industry in Bosnia and Herzegovina, *International Journal of Business and Administrative Studies*, 8(2), 48-62.

Park, Sunyoung and Kim. Eun-Jee (2019). Organizational culture, **leaders' vision** of talent,

> and HR functions on career changers' commitment: the moderating effect of training in South Korea, *Asia Pacific Journal of Human Resources*, 57(3), 345-368.

Parsons, Paul (2017), editor, *30-Seconds Theories*, New York, Metro Books.

Pearce II, John A. and Robinson, Jr., Richard B. (2004). *Strategic Management,* Illinois: Richard

> D. Irwin, Inc.

Penney, Christopher et al (2019). An Image Theory of Strategic Decision-Making in Family

Pew Research Center,

> https://www.pewresearch.org/hispanic/2021/11/04/majority-of-latinos-say-skin-

> Businesses, *Journal of Family Business Management*, 9(4), 451-467.

Pieper, Torsten M. et al (2021). Update 2021 Family Business' Contribution to the U. Economy,

> https://familyenterpriseusa.com/wp-content/uploads/2021/02/Family-Businesses-Contribution-to-the-US-Economy_v.01272021-FINAL_4.pdf.

Pihie, Zal et al (2014). Entrepreneurial Leadership Practices and School Innovativeness, *Sourth*

> *African Journal of Education*, 34(1), 1-22.

Porter, Michael E. (1998). The Competitive Advantage of Nations, New York, the Free

> Press.

Prahalad, C. K. and Hamel, Gary (1990). The Core Competence of the Corporation,

> Harvard Business Review, (68) 3, 80.

Pride, William M. et al (2023). *Foundation of Business*, Boston: MA, Cengage Learning, Inc.

Quach, Sara et al (2021). The experience of regret in small business failure: who's to blame?,
    European Journal of marketing, 55(8), 2201-2238.

Rahman, Md H. and Murullah, Sheikh M. (2014). Motivational Need Hierarchy of Employees in
    Public and Private Commercial Banks *Central European Business Review*, 3(2), 44-53.

Ramos, Maria et al (2011). Family values and the family business in northeast Mexico,
    Cuadernos de Administración, 24(42).
    Rantanen, Kalevi and Domb, Ellen (2002). *Simplified TRIZ,*
    Baca Raton; Florida, Sr. Lucie Press.

Rao, T. V. and Vijayalakshmi, M (2000). Organization Development, *Organization Development*
    Journal, 18(1), 51-63.

Riordan, Diane A. and Riordan, Michael P. (1993). Field Theory: An Alternative to Systems
    Theories in Understanding the Small Family Business, *Journal of Small Business Management,* 31(2), 66.

Rivard, Suzanne (2020). Theory Building is neither an Art nor a Science. It is a craft. *Journal of*
    Information Technology, https://journals.sagepub.com/doi/10.1177/0268396220911938.

Robbins, Stephen P (1993). *Organizational Behavior*, Englewood Cliffs; New Jersey, Prentice-
    Hall, Inc.

Robbins, Stephen P. and Coulter, Mary (2014). *Management*, Boston: Pearson
    Education, Inc.

Robinson, Martin et al (2021). Nothing so Practical as Theory: A Rapid View of the Use of
    Behaviour Change Theory in Family Planning Interventions Involving Men and Boys, *Reproductive Health*, 18(1), 1-28.

Rock, David (2009). Managing with the Brain in Mind, Strategy + Business, vol. 56, pp. 59-67.

Rosa, Nelly T. R. (2009). From a Family-owned to a Family-controlled Business:
> Applying Chandler's Insights to Explain Family Business Transitional Stages, *Journal of Management History*, 15(3), 284-298.

Rothaermel, Frank T.(2015). *Strategic Management*, New York: Ny, McGraw-Hill Education;

Ruben, Brent D. and Gigliotti, Ralph A. (2021). Explaining incongruities between leadership
> theory and practice: integrating theories of resonance, communication and systems,
> *Leadership & Organizational Development Journal*, 42(6), 942-957.

Ruchti, Bruno and Livotov, Pavel (2001). *TRIZ-based Innovation Principles and a Process for*
> *Problems Solving in Business and Management*, TRIZ Journal.

Sadiq, Fawad et al (2021). Managers' Disruptive Innovation Activities: the Construct,
> Measurement and Validity, *Management Decisions*, 59(2), 153-174.

Salazar, Mary K. (1991). Comparison of Four Behavioral Theories, *AAOHN Journal*, 39(3), 128-
> 138.

Schmidts, Torsten and Shepherd, Deborah (2015). Social Identity and family Business:
> Exploring Family Social Capital, *Journal of Family Business Management*, 5(2).

Sedrine, Sinda B. et al (2021). Leadership Style Effect on Virtual Team efficiency: Trust,
> Operational Cohesion and Media Richness Roles, *Journal of Management Development*, 40(5), 365-388.

Sethuraman, Kavitha and Suresh, Jayshree (2014). Effective Leadership Styles, *International*
> *Business Research*, 7(9), 165-172. The five major functions of leadership are categorized as follows (Joel DiGirolamo, 2010).

Si, Steven et al (2021). Disruptive innovation, business model and sharing economy: the bike-
>sharing cases in China, *Management Decisions*, 59(11), 2674-2692.

Siliconindia (February 10, 2014).
>https://www.siliconindia.com/news/business/indias-10-oldest-family-owned-businesses-nid-161014-cid-3.html.

Simon, David G. and Hitt, Michael A. (2003). Managing Resources: linking Unique Resources,
>Management, and Wealth Creation in Family Firms, *Entrepreneurship: Theory &*
>*Practice*, 27(4), 339-358

Simpeh, Kwabena > (2011). Entrepreneurship Theories and Empirical Research: A Summary
>Review of the Literature, European Journal of Business and Management, 3(6),1-8.

Skandalis, Konstantinos and Ghazzawi, Issam A. (2014). Immigration and Entrepreneurship in
>Greece: Factors Influencing and Shaping Entrepreneurship Establishments by Immigrants, *International Journal of Entrepreneurship*, 18, 77-100.

Skopak, Adi and Hadzaihetovie, Nereida (2022). The Impact of Transformational and
>Transactional Leadership Style on Employee Job Satisfaction, *International Journal of Business and Administrative Studies*, 8(3), 113-126.

Soewarno, Noorlailie et al (2019). Green Innovation Strategy and Green Innovation: The Roles
>of Green Organizational Identity and Environmental Organizational legitimacy, 57(11), 3061-3078.

Soni. Alisha and Kanupriya, Misra B. (2021). Personality traits and entrepreneurial intention
>among Chartered Accountancy students, *Problems and Perspectives in Management*, 19(3), 136-147.

Suarez-Barraza, Manuel F. and Miguel Davila, Jose A. (2021). Exploring Fayol's Management
>Process in a Traditional Mayan Dance (Pochó Dance):

an Ethnographic Study, *Asia-Pacific Journal of Business Administration*, 13(2), 189-215.

Suess-Reyes, Julia (2017). Understanding the Transgenerational Orientation of Family
Businesses: the Role of Family Governance and Business Family Identity, *Zeitschrift für Betriebswirtschaft*, 87(6), 749-777.

Summera, Malik et al (2020) Entrepreneurial leadership and Employee Innovative Behaviour in
Software Industry, *Journal of Business & Economic, 12(1), 63-76.*

Sundararajan, Malavika and Sundararajan, Binod (2015). Immigrant Capital and Entrepreneurial
Opportunities, *Entrepreneurial Business and Economics Review*, 3(3), 29-50.

Swanson, Richard A. and Chermack, Thomas J. (2013). *Theory Building in Applied Disciplines*,
Berrett- Koehler Publishing Company, San Francisco: California.

Tabor, William et al (2020). The Effects of Spiritual Leadership in Family Firms: A
Tests of Fayol's theory Conclusion, *Enterprises of Histoire*, 34, 98-107.
Conservation of Resources Perspective, *Journal of Business Ethics*, 163(4), 729-743.

Tartell, Rose (2016). Understand Teams by Using the GRPI Model, *Training*, 53(1), 22-27.

Thomas, Joseph J (2010). Bet You Never Heard of this Leadership Trait, *Journal of Leadership*
Education, 9(2), 1-3.

Thompson, Arthur A. (2020). *Strategy: Core Concepts and Analytical Approaches*,
Boston: McGraw-Hill Irwin, Inc.

Torraco, Richard J. (2008). Theory Building Research Methods in Swanson Richard A. and
Holton III, Elwood F., editors, *Human Resource Development Research Handbook*, San Francisco, Berrett-Koehler

Publishers.

United Nations (2020), *Peace, Dignity, and Equality on Healthy planet,*
https://www.un.org/en/global-issues/migration

USA Facts:
https://usafacts.org/issues/immigration. Uploaded in February 2022.

Uslu, Osman (2019). A General Overview of Leadership Theories from a Critical Perspective,
Marketing and Management of Innovations, 1, 161-172.

Valdés, Gonzalo et al (2021). Barriers to Innovation and Willingness to Innovate in the Food
Sector: the Case of Chile, *Food Journal*, 123(10), 3344-3357.

Van den Berghe, L.A.A. and Carchon, Steven (2003). Agency Relations within the Family
Business System: An Exploratory Approach, *Corporate Governance*, 11(3), 171-179.

Vandor, Peter (2021). Research: Why Immigrants are More Likely to Become Entrepreneurs,
https://hbr.org/2021/08/research-why-immmigrants-are-more-likely.

Visser, Thea and van Scheers, Louise (2018). Can Family Business Managers manage Family?
Business Risks? *Journal of Contemporary Management Issues*, 23(1), 123-137.

Volkema, Roger J. and Kapoutsis, Illias (2016). From Restaurants to Board Rooms: How
Initiating Negotiations Teaches Management Principles and Theory, *Journal of
Management Education*, 40(1), 76-101.

Vrontis, Demetris (2019). Entrepreneurial Exploration and Exploitation Processes of Family
Businesses in the Food Sector, *British Food Journal*, 121(11), 2759-2779.

Wacker, John G. (1998). A Definition of Theory: Research Guidelines for Different Theory-

Building Research Methods in Operations Management, *Journal of Operations Management*, 16(4), 361-385.

Wagner-Tsukamoto, Sigmund (2008). Scientific Management revisited: Did Taylorism fail
because of a too positive image of human nature? *Journal of Management History*, 14(4), 348-372.

Wang, Can et al (2021). The Business Strategy, Competitive Advantage and Financial
Strategy: A Perspective from Corporate Maturity Mismatched Investment, *Journal of Competitiveness*, 13(1), 164-181.

Wang, Rong (2020). Marginality and Team Building in Collaborative Crowdsourcing, *Online
Information Review*, 44(4), 827-846.

Weinreich, Simon et al (2022). Methodology for Managing Disruptive Innovation by Value-
Oriented Portfolio Planning, *Journal of Open Innovation*, 8(1), 48.

Wheelen, Thomas L. and Hunger, David J. (2002). *Strategic Management and Business Policy,*
Massachusetts: Addison-Wesley Publishing Company.

Whetten, David A. and Cameron, Kim S. (2020). *Developing Management Skills*, Pearson
Education, Inc.

Williams, Chuck (2022). *Management*, Boston: MA, Cengage Learning, Inc.

Witzel, Morgen (2002). Parkinson and Peter A-Z of Management Principles, *Financial Times*,
p.14.

Wolf, Victoria et al (2021). Innovation strategies in the context of the paradigm of the five
dimensions of innovation strategy, *LogForum*, 17(2), 205-211).

Wren, Daniel A. (2003). The Influence of Henri Fayol on Management Theory and education in
North America: Early Recognition and the Coubrough Translation, 2. The Storrs' Translation and Management Education in North America, 3. Renewed Interest and

Empirical

Wu, Mengyun et al (2020). Successor Selection in Family Business Using Theory of Planned
> Behaviour and Cognitive Dimension of Social Capital Theory: Evidence from Ghana, *Journal of Small Business and Enterprise Development*, 27(6), 905-926.

Xu, Kunlin et al (2019). Immigrant entrepreneurs and their cross-cultural capabilities: A study of
> Chinese immigrant entrepreneurs in Australia, *Journal of International Entrepreneurship*, 17(4), 520-557.

Ya-long, Wel et al (2018). Is Business Planning Useful for the New Venture Emergence?:
> Moderated by the Innovativeness of Products, Chinese Management Studies, 12(4), 847-870.

Yitshaki, Ronit et al (2022). The Role of Compassion in Shaping Social Entrepreneurs' Prosocial
> Opportunity Recognition, *Journal of Business Ethics*, 179(2), 617-647.

Yunus, Md Ridzwan B. and et al (2018). The Importance Role of Personality Trait, *International*
> *Journal of Academic Research in Business & Social Sciences*, 8(7), 1-28-1036.

Zhang, Ying et al (2020). Designing Creative Teams from Creative Members: The Role of
> Reward Interdependence and Knowledge Sharing, *Nankai Business Review International*, 11(4), 617-634.

Zhou, Yu et al (2017). On Participation Constrained Team Formation, *Journal of Computer*
> *Science and Technology*, 32(1), 139-154.

Zhu, Jessica and Pulleyblank, William (2020). Determining a Positive Causal Relationship of
> Immigration on Living Standards, *Journal of International Migration and Integration*,
> 21(4), 1043-1056.

Zou, Wen-Jie et al (2014). Performance Appraisals Between Family Business and Non-family
> Businesses, *International Journal of Organizational*

Innovation, 7(1), 36-45.

Zygmunt, Aleksandra (2022). The Effect of Research and Development Personnel on Innovation

Activities of Firms: Evidence from Small and Medium-sized Enterprises from the Visegrad Group countries.

www.ingramcontent.com/pod-product-compliance
Lightning Source LLC
Chambersburg PA
CBHW052111030426
42335CB00025B/2927